THE COMPLETE
WINDOWS 10
PRIVACY GUIDE

MARTIN BRINKMANN

FALL CREATORS
UPDATE EDITION

DEDICATION

For Julia. This book would not exist without your moral support
and understanding. Thank you, my love.

CONTENTS

FOREWORD

Privacy is a hot topic in today's connected world. This is true especially when it comes to user tracking on the Internet, but also tracking built-in to operating systems such as Windows 10 or Android, or programs such as Google Chrome or Mozilla Firefox.

Windows 10 has probably been the operating system that Microsoft has been attacked the most for from privacy advocates and concerned users in regards to privacy and data collection.

Probably the biggest factors for this are changes made to Telemetry collecting on the operating system, a lack of transparency when it comes to the collecting of data, and a lack of distinction between data that Microsoft collects, and data that is required by services or applications for functionality.

Questions about which data is collected when Windows 10 is used, why it is collected, where it is stored, and how it is used or shared, are not answered to the satisfaction of privacy advocates or users who are concerned about privacy.

> A significant issue is the telemetry data the company receives. While Microsoft insists that it aggregates and anonymizes this data, it hasn't explained just how it does so. Microsoft also won't say how long this data is retained, instead providing only general timeframes.[1]

Microsoft made concessions to that with the release of the Windows 10 Creators Update when it revealed what the Basic[2] and Full Telemetry[3] settings mean in terms of data collecting.

It is clear that the data that is collected is important to Microsoft, as it uses it to detect and resolve issues, and to find ways to optimize the operating system. The new faster release scheme with two feature updates per year demands a closer look on data as well, to prioritize development for instance or recognize issues more quickly.

Data is required for some functionality as well. The digital assistant Cortana for instance requires access to the device's location, data from emails and text messages, the call history, contacts you have and how often you interact with those contacts, and the apps you use.

---

[1] https://www.eff.org/deeplinks/2016/08/windows-10-microsoft-blatantly-disregards-user-choice-and-privacy-deep-dive

[2] https://docs.microsoft.com/en-us/windows/configuration/basic-level-windows-diagnostic-events-and-fields

[3] https://docs.microsoft.com/en-us/windows/configuration/windows-diagnostic-data

Windows 10 users can opt-out of most of the data collecting, but even if they turn any preference off during setup or under the Privacy section of the Settings application, data still gets collected and transferred to Microsoft.

The rise of privacy programs for Windows 10[4] is a response to Microsoft's inability to respond to concerns adequately, for instance by making it difficult to control data collection and submission to Microsoft.

More than a dozen programs have been created that perform all kinds of pro-privacy operations on the operating system when executed.

All offer options to tweak privacy settings, and many to remove Windows apps, block Microsoft servers, or disable Windows scheduled tasks or Services.

This guide

This privacy guide covers every aspect of Windows 10 privacy and data collecting in detail. It includes information on all privacy settings that are exposed to users in the Settings application and other system locations, and explains in simple but detailed terms what each does.

The guide looks at Microsoft's stance on privacy, provides you with resources to do your own research on the topic, and comes with a 5-minute privacy improvement guide to make the most important privacy related changes right away so that you don't have to read the entire book first before you make the most important changes in regards to privacy.

It looks at differences between Windows 10 Editions, the installation process, reviews privacy programs created for Windows 10, and at specific features of the operating system and how data collecting plays a role for these features.

---

[4] https://www.ghacks.net/2015/08/14/comparison-of-windows-10-privacy-tools/

WHAT MICROSOFT SAYS ABOUT PRIVACY AND WINDOWS 10

Microsoft published a post with the title **Privacy and Windows 10**[5] back in September 2015 on the official Windows Experience Blog to address rising privacy concerns.

According to Terry Myerson, Executive Vice President, Windows and Devices Group, Microsoft designed Windows 10 with two "straightforward privacy principles" in mind.

> Windows 10 collects information so the product will work better for you.

> You are in control with the ability to determine what information is collected.

Myerson goes on to explain that Microsoft thinks of data that the company does and does not collect in three different levels:

1. **Safety and Reliability data** – This data is collected to "provide a secure and reliable experience". It includes data such as an anonymous device ID, device type, and application crash data which Microsoft and its developer partners use to improve application reliability.
2. **Personalization data** – This data is used to provide users with a custom experience, for instance by providing text completion suggestions, using the digital assistant Cortana, or giving users updates on game scores when their favorite teams play.
3. **Advertising data that Microsoft does not collect** – Microsoft won't collect content of emails or other communications, or files, to deliver targeted advertising.

In 2017, Myerson published two additional privacy focused articles on the Windows 10 Experience blog.

The new Privacy Dashboard was announced in the first entitled **Our continuing commitment to your privacy with Windows 10**[6]. The new online dashboard[7] provides options to Windows users who sign in to Windows using a Microsoft Account to control activity data that is collected by Microsoft products such as Windows 10.

Microsoft announced as well that it would improve the privacy part of the setup experience, simplify diagnostic data levels, and reduce data collected at the Basic level (of Telemetry).

---

[5] https://blogs.windows.com/windowsexperience/2015/09/28/privacy-and-windows-10/

[6] https://blogs.windows.com/windowsexperience/2017/01/10/continuing-commitment-privacy-windows-10/

[7] https://account.microsoft.com/privacy

> First, we will introduce a new set up experience for you to choose the settings that are right for you.
>
> This experience, which replaces previous Express Settings, will look slightly different depending on the version of Windows you are using. If you are moving from Windows 7 or Windows 8, or doing a fresh install of Windows 10, the new set up experience will clearly show you simple but important settings and you will need to choose your settings before you can move forward with setup.
>
> If you are already using Windows 10, we will use notifications to prompt you to choose your privacy settings.

Microsoft made the decision to reduce Telemetry levels from three to two configurable levels in the Settings application of the Windows 10 Creators Update version. The company removed the Enhanced level, leaving Basic and Full as the two remaining options during Setup and in the Settings application.

Myerson confirmed that Microsoft reduced the data that is collected when the Basic level is enabled.

> We use this data to help keep Windows and apps secure, up-to-date, and running properly when you let Microsoft know the capabilities of your device, what is installed, and whether Windows is operating correctly. This option also includes basic error reporting back to Microsoft.

Three months later, in April 2017, Myerson published **Windows 10 privacy journey continues: more transparency and controls for you**[8] on the Windows Experience blog.

In it he revealed three enhancements to privacy on Windows 10.

- In-product information improvements by adding short descriptions and learn more links to privacy settings to help customers better understand each.
- An update to the Microsoft Privacy statement to include more information about the privacy changes in the Creators Update.
- Publication of more information about the data that Microsoft collects.

Marisa Rogers, WDG Privacy Officer, revealed[9] in September 2017 on the official Windows Experience blog that privacy enhancements were coming to the Windows 10 Fall Creators Update.

---

[8] https://blogs.windows.com/windowsexperience/2017/04/05/windows-10-privacy-journey-continues-more-transparency-and-controls-for-you/

[9] https://blogs.windows.com/windowsexperience/2017/09/13/privacy-enhancements-coming-to-the-windows-10-fall-creators-update/

She listed three improvements in the article:

1. Direct access to the privacy statement during setup, and links next to the available privacy settings during setup that lead to the privacy statement paragraph that refers to it.
2. Permission prompts not only for location data but also other data that Windows Store applications request such as camera, microphone, contacts, or calendar.
3. A new Window Analytics setting for Enterprise customers.

PRIVACY OPTIONS DURING SETUP

Windows 10 users and administrators have only one option when it comes to setting up the operating system. Previous versions of Windows 10 shipped with two – Express and Custom – but Microsoft changed the experience in Windows 10 version 1703.

This means that it is no longer required to hunt down the "custom" link during setup to get more control, and customize some of the privacy options that Microsoft added as options to the Windows 10 setup process.

The following screens are captures of Windows 10 version 1709 – The Fall Creators Update. Note that Microsoft changed the setup experience in that version, and that the screens will have different options when you install an earlier version of Windows 10.

Setup provides Windows users with control over two privacy related options.

The most important part of setup from a privacy perspective is the privacy settings screen of the setup. It lists important privacy options that are enabled by default. You may disable those during setup, or after setup when you open the Privacy hub of the Settings application.

Note that you may disable only a limited number of privacy related options during setup or first run; the privacy hub lists way more options, and it is highly suggested that you go through the listing there at least once to configure each setting accordingly.

One chapter of this book walks you through all the preferences that you find there.

The second option that users get during setup or first run is that they may set up a Microsoft account or a local account (Microsoft calls it offline account during setup) for use on the system.

This is important as well, as features may be limited to a certain account type.

Note that the following pages concentrate on privacy options only. Most screens of the setup are self-explanatory and are not related to privacy.

Account

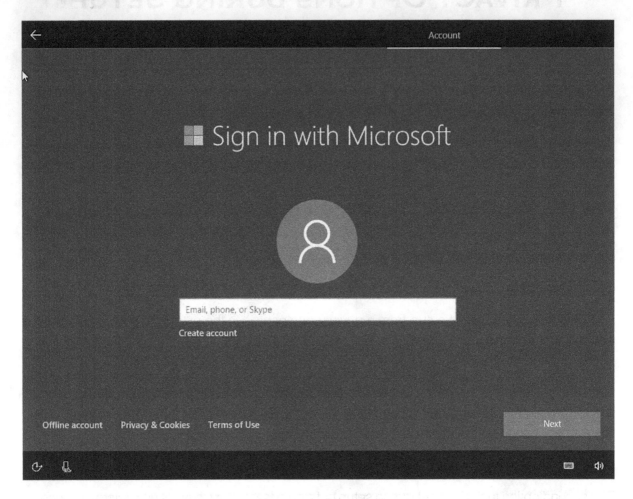

The Account setup page gives you two options:

1. Use a Microsoft Account
2. Use a local (offline) account.

I suggest you check out the comparison in a later chapter of this book for detailed information on local accounts and Microsoft accounts.

The core differences between local accounts and Microsoft accounts are the following ones:

- Local accounts are active on a single machine only.
- A Microsoft account may be used on multiple devices.
- Some account preferences may be synced across devices if a Microsoft account is used to sign in. This includes themes, language preferences, passwords, or Internet Explorer settings. This is enabled by default.

- Some features on Windows 10 require a Microsoft Account. This is the case for OneDrive for instance, the default file synchronization service.
- You can reset the Microsoft Account password online.
- A Microsoft Account is no longer required to download (free) Store applications if you use Windows 10 Pro or Enterprise. You still need a Microsoft account to download Store apps on Windows 10 Home .
- You may use a Microsoft account to sign up and use other Microsoft company products, especially online products.

Microsoft links to privacy & help information, and the terms of use on the first page of setup as well.

Generally speaking, a Microsoft Account is more convenient in some regards, but it does link the account to the device and comes with data synchronization enabled by default.

Cortana

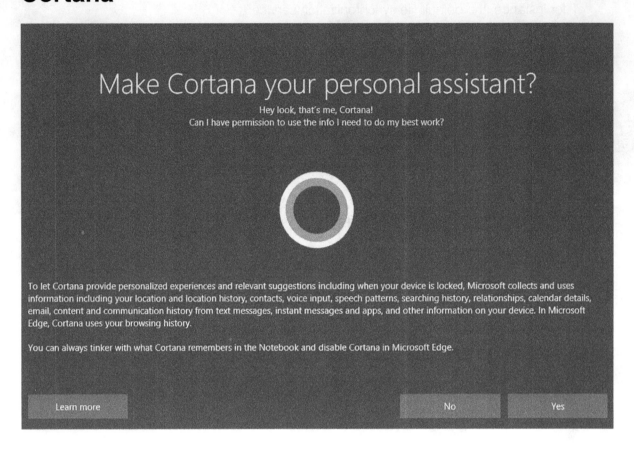

Cortana is a digital personal assistant that Microsoft introduced in Windows 10. You may communicate with Cortana using speech or text, and may use it for a variety of purposes.

Some of these include running searches, setting up reminders, getting answers to direct questions (What's the weather), reserving tables, composing emails, and a lot more.

Cortana requires access to data for that, and Microsoft "collects and uses information" for that purposes.

> .. including your location and location history, contacts, voice input, speech patterns, searching history, relationships, calendar details, email, content and communication history from text messages, instant messages and apps, and other information on your device. In Microsoft Edge, Cortana uses your browsing history.

You may select the "no" option on the setup page to deny Cortana's permissions request. You may change what Cortana is allowed to do later on as well.

Services

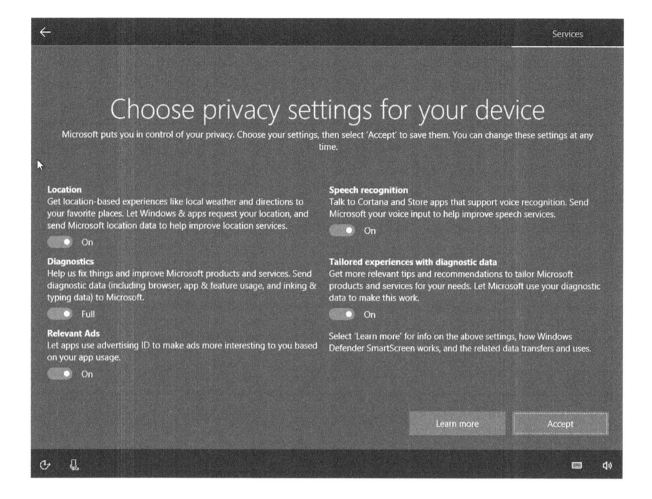

The Services setup page lists all privacy related settings and descriptions of the setup process. They are enabled by default, and just some of the privacy settings that Windows 10 ships with.

Please note that you can change the status of any of the services listed on the page later on as well.

Location – This setting determines whether applications and Windows may request access to the location of the device for functionality. Two apps that make use of location are the weather application, and Maps.

Location data is sent to Microsoft and used to improve location services according to the description. Microsoft may share location data with trusted partners for that.

° Microsoft's location service provides location information to Windows devices using a combination of global positioning service (GPS), nearby wireless access points, cell towers, and your IP address, depending on the capabilities of your device.

- ° Turning on Location enables certain apps, services, and Windows features to ask for permission to access and use your location data to deliver location-aware services at as precise a level as your device supports. When your location is used by a location-aware app or service, your location information and recent location history is stored on your device and sent to Microsoft in a de-identified format to improve location services.
- ° In addition, if you are logged in with your Microsoft account, your last known good location information is saved to the cloud and available to other apps or services using your Microsoft account across devices. If your device cannot obtain a good location on its own (like for example in a building or basement), it can use your last known good location stored in the cloud.
- ° You can turn off location access and clear your device's location history at any time in Start > Settings > Privacy > Location.
- ° If you have a portable device, such as a laptop, turning on location will also enable the Find my Device feature, which uses your location data to help you find your device if you lose it. For this feature to work, you must log into Windows with your Microsoft Account. You can turn this off at any time in Start > Settings > Update & Security > Find my Device.

Diagnostics – Diagnostic data is sent to Microsoft. This includes information on browser, application and feature use, inking and typing data, and more.

Check the Telemetry chapter for detailed information on what gets collected and sent to Microsoft. This feature cannot be turned off, but you can switch from full to basic Telemetry during setup.

- ° Diagnostic data helps identify and troubleshoot problems, and keep the device up to data and secure.
- ° The data is transmitted to Microsoft, and stored with one or multiple unique identifiers that Microsoft uses to recognize individual users or devices.
- ° There are two levels of diagnostic that can be set during setup: full or basic.
- ° Basic data is data that is vital to the operation of Windows. It provides Microsoft with information on the device's capabilities, installed software, and if Windows operates correctly.
- ° Full data includes all Basic data, and information on app and browser usage, feature usage, how long apps are used, which services you use to sign in to apps, or how often Windows Help and Support is used. The memory state of the device is transferred to Microsoft at the full data level. Microsoft notes that any identifying information is removed from the typed and handwritten input data.
- ° Microsoft uses the data to improve products and services for all Windows users. It won't use the data to personalize Microsoft products or services, unless you allow Microsoft to do so.
- ° You can adjust the diagnostic data level in Start > Settings > Privacy > Feedback & diagnostics

Relevant ads – Windows 10 may use an advertising ID, a unique identifier, to personalize advertisement on the operating system.

Advertisement is based on application usage if the setting is enabled. If you turn it off, ads are still displayed but they are not personalized anymore using the advertising ID.

- ° Windows generates a unique advertising ID for each user on a device. This ID may be used by application developers and advertising networks for personalized advertisement.
- ° Microsoft compares the use of the advertising ID to the use of cookies by websites.
- ° You can turn this off in Start > Settings > Privacy at any time.

Speech recognition – Cortana, the digital assistant requires speech recognition if you want to use voice commands and interact with Cortana using voice. Similarly, Store apps may also support voice recognition and require it as well.

Voice input data is sent to Microsoft to help improve speech services. If you turn this off, you cannot communicate with Cortana or other applications using voice. This does not impact the functionality of connected microphones though.

- ° Windows provides both a device based speech recognition feature (available through the Windows Speech Recognition desktop app), and a cloud based speech recognition service that was introduced alongside Cortana in those markets and regions where Cortana is available.
- ° Turning on the Speech recognition setting allows Microsoft to collect and use your voice recordings to provide you with cloud-based speech recognition services in Cortana, supported Store apps, and over time in other parts of Windows.
- ° Microsoft collects information from the user dictionary as part of the service. The user dictionary stores unique words like names you write, which help users type and ink more accurately.
- ° Both the voice data and the user dictionary are used by Microsoft to improve the ability to correctly recognize user speech.
- ° You can turn off this feature at any time in Start > Settings > Privacy > Speech, inking & typing.

Tailored experiences with diagnostic data – Microsoft may use diagnostic data to display tips and recommendations to users.

- ° Microsoft will use some diagnostic data to "personalize your experiences with Windows and other products and services". This includes, according to Microsoft, suggestions on how to customize and optimize Windows: and recommendations and offers of Windows features and supported apps, services, hardware, and peripherals.

- This feature powers campaigns that suggest apps to users that do things better than others, according to Microsoft. Chrome or Firefox users may get Edge recommended to them for instance.
- Microsoft may also suggest trying OneDrive for storage, or purchase more space on OneDrive, or give Office 365 a try.
- Full includes additional information, e.g. the use of browsers or applications.
- Tailored experiences won't use crash, speech, typing, or inking input data for personalization.
- You can turn this off in Start > Settings > Privacy > Feedback & diagnostics.

5-MINUTE PRIVACY CONFIGURATION

This book offers a lot of information when it comes to privacy, Windows configuration and related topics of interest.

This 5-minute guide is designed to make the most important privacy-related changes right away without having to read for hours what each setting does.

I recommend that you read through the rest of the book, but since it may take a while, you may want to make some changes as quickly as possible.

The following settings concentrate on two things: setting Telemetry data collecting to Basic, the lowest available level (unless you run Enterprise, Education or IoT editions of Windows), and turning off features that may display suggestions/advertisement.

Let's start:

1. Use the shortcut Windows-I to open the Settings application.
2. Go to Privacy > Feedback & Diagnostics.
3. Set the diagnostic and usage data level to Basic.
4. Set "Let Microsoft provide tailored experiences with relevant tips and recommendations by using your diagnostic data" to off.
5. Go to General using the left sidebar.
6. Set "Let apps use advertising ID to make ads more interesting to you based on your app usage (turning this off will reset your ID) to off.
7. Set "Show me suggested content in the Settings app" to off.
8. Go to Personalization > Lock Screen.
9. Set "Get fun facts, tips, tricks, and more on your lock screen" to off.
10. Go to Start using the left sidebar.
11. Set "Occasionally show suggestions in Start" to off.
12. Go to System > Notifications & actions
13. Set "get tips, tricks, and suggestions as you use Windows" to off.
14. Set "Show me the Windows welcome experience after updates and occasionally when I sign in to highlight what's new and suggested" to off.
15. Go to Accounts > Sync your Settings.
16. Set "Sync settings" to off, unless you want your settings to sync to the cloud. If you do, disable all data sets on the same page that you don't require instead.

17. Go to Updates & security > Advanced options > Choose how updates are delivered, and set "download Windows updates and apps from other PCs.." to off, and "get updates from Microsoft.." to PCs on my local network.
18. Open File Explorer.
19. Select File > Change folder and search options.
20. Switch to the View tab.
21. Disable "show sync provider notifications".

Configuring Privacy Settings After Setup

You can configure any of the privacy settings that were displayed to you during setup afterwards as well; plus, a lot more that were not exposed during setup.

This part of the guide looks at Privacy options in the Windows 10 Settings application. For detailed information on privacy options not listed under Settings, check out the following chapters as you find those there, as well as options that are not in Settings > Privacy, and information on Group Policy and Registry settings.

You start the Settings application either with a click on Start > Settings, or by using the keyboard shortcut Windows-I.

Open the Privacy section once the Settings application opens.

Note: Some features come with a default list of applications that are allowed to use that feature. This list may vary slightly from region to region.

It is a good idea to go through these listings to disable permissions for applications that you don't plan on using, or don't want to have access to a feature.

Privacy → General

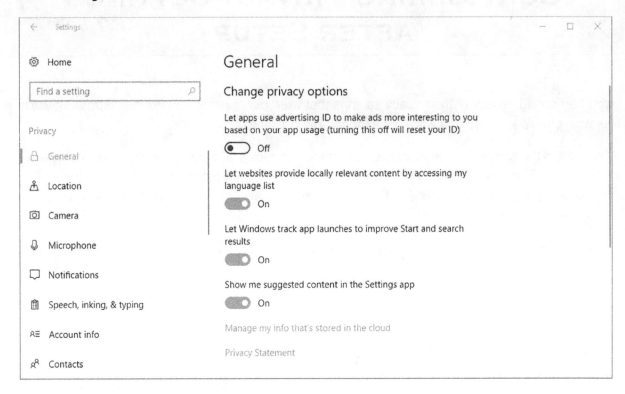

This is the start page of the Privacy category of the Settings application. You find the following options here:

- **Let apps use advertising ID to make ads more interesting to you based on your app usage (turning this off will reset your ID).** If you have disabled the option during setup, it is already set to off. Turning this to off results in non-personalized ads, but not fewer ads. Basically, what this means is that Microsoft creates no profile of your interests to use it to display advertisement to you.
- **Let websites provide locally relevant content by accessing my language list.** Websites may look up supported languages to customize content based on those.
- **Let Windows track app launches to improve Start and search results.** If this is turned on, Windows maintains a list of most used apps that it displays to you in Start and when running searches.
- **Show me suggested content in the Settings app**. Windows 10 may display suggestions in the Settings application.

Privacy → Location

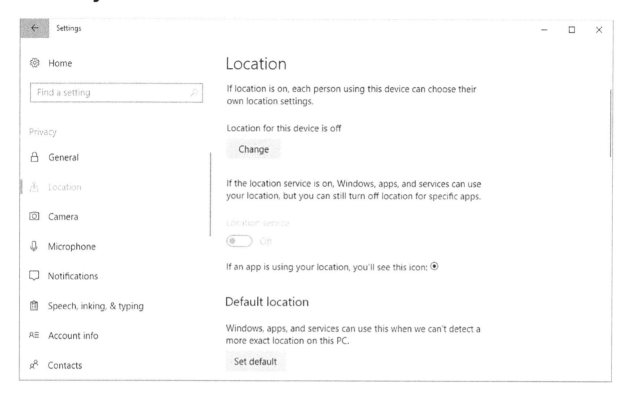

The Location settings allow you to manage location-based features and functionality. Location may be used by applications such as Maps or Weather for personalized results. You find the following options here:

- **Change the status of the device's location feature**. You can turn the location feature on or off here for the device. This setting was part of Setup as well.
- **Set a default location**. Windows uses the default location for its functionality, and apps may use it as well, if a more exact location cannot be detected.
- **Manage and clear the location history**. Location history is stored on the device for a limited time. Apps and Windows may use it if the location cannot be determined otherwise.
- **Choose apps that may use location**. You may enable or disable location use for applications individually as well if Location is enabled. Works only if location is enabled. The following apps are configured to use Location:

    ○ Camera
    ○ Cortana
    ○ Mail and Calendar
    ○ Maps
    ○ Messaging

- ° Microsoft Edge
- ° News
- ° Twitter
- ° Weather

- Control Geofencing – using location data to see when you cross in or out of a boundary drawn around a place of interest.

Privacy → Camera

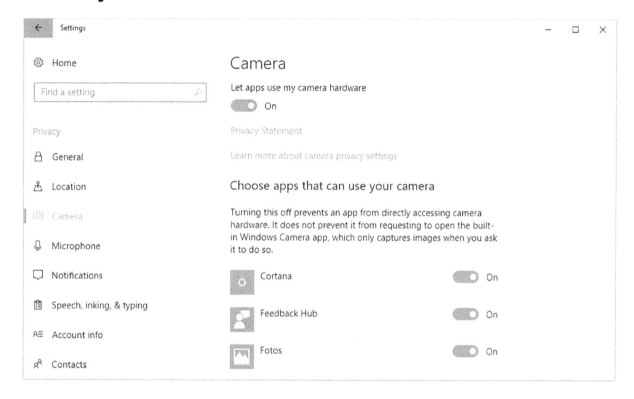

Camera lets you control whether applications may use camera hardware, a connected webcam for instance. The following options are provided:

- **Let apps use my camera hardware**. You can turn the feature on or off here for the device. Note that turning it off here won't impact the use of the camera in desktop programs.
- Choose apps that may use the camera. You may prevent select applications from using the camera. This works only if camera is enabled on the device. The following applications are listed by default:

  ○ Cortana
  ○ Feedback Hub
  ○ Fotos
  ○ Maps
  ○ Microsoft Edge
  ○ OneNote
  ○ Skype
  ○ Store
  ○ Twitter

Privacy → Microphone

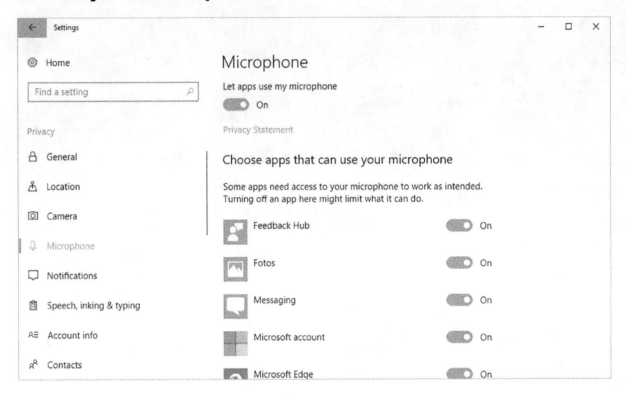

Microphone works identical to the Camera option, only that it controls connected microphones. The following options are available:

- **Let apps use my microphone**. You may enable or disable the use of the microphone by apps here. Note that turning this off won't impact microphone use in desktop programs.
- Choose apps that may use the microphone. You can prevent select applications from using the microphone. The microphone feature needs to be enabled for this to work. The following applications are listed there by default:

    - Feedback Hub
    - Fotos
    - Messaging
    - Microsoft accounts
    - Microsoft Edge
    - OneNote
    - Skype
    - Store
    - Take a Test
    - Twitter

    - Voice Recorder
    - Xbox
    - Xbox Game bar

Privacy → Notifications

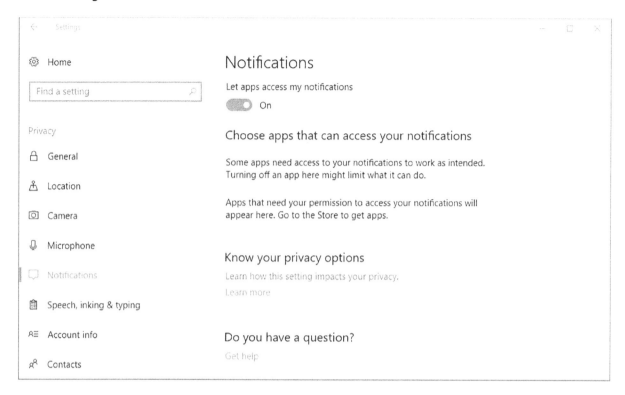

This page provides you with options to disable access to notifications by applications. The following options are provided:

- **Let apps access my notifications**. This enables or disables the notifications system for applications system wide.
- Choose apps that can use notifications. If notifications are enabled, you may use this setting to prevent select applications from using notifications.

Windows 10 Fall Creators Update ships without apps that are permitted to access notifications on the device.

Privacy → Speech, inking and typing

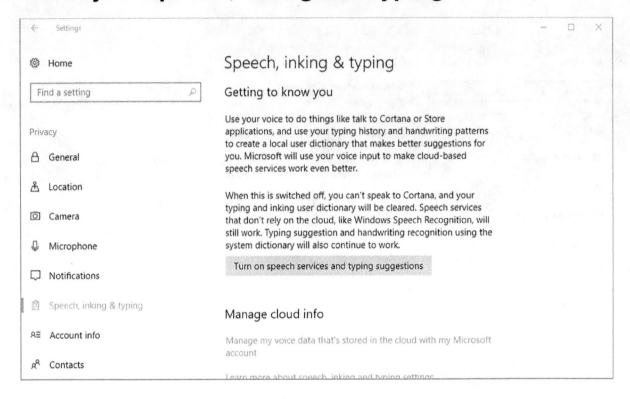

You may change the status of speech services and typing suggestions on this page. The following options are provided:

- **Turn speech services and suggestions on or off**. If you turn this off, you cannot speak to Cortana anymore, and the personal user dictionary will be cleared. This won't impact speech services that don't rely on the cloud.

You may also follow the "manage my voice data that's stored in the cloud with my Microsoft account" link to manage voice data on the web.[10]

---

[10] https://account.microsoft.com/privacy

Privacy → Account Info

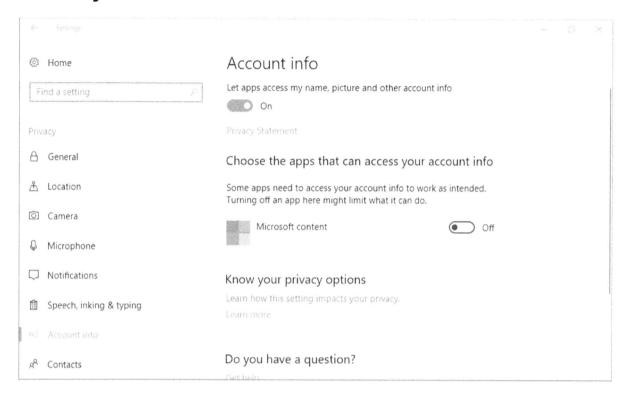

Here you may select whether apps may access account related information such as your name or picture. The following options are provided on this page:

- **Let apps access my name, picture and other account info**.
- Turn off access to Account information for select applications. Note that this works only if Account Info is turned on.

The following applications are listed under Account Info automatically:

- Microsoft content

Privacy → Contacts

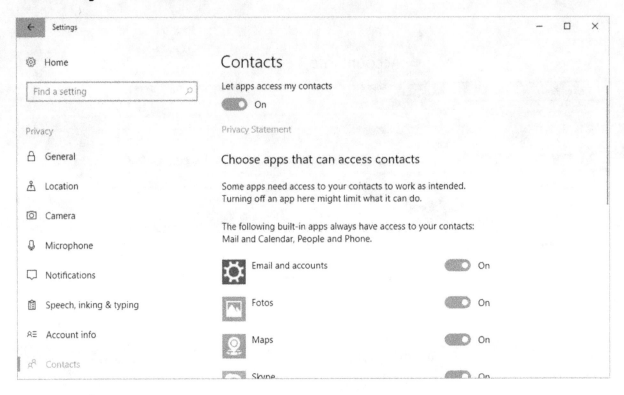

The Contacts privacy settings allow you to define whether applications may access contacts on the device. Some apps, Mail and Calendar, People and Phone, have access to contacts even if the feature is turned off. The following options are provided:

- **Let apps access my contacts.** This setting determines whether Windows Store applications may access contacts if you allow them do to so (or if Windows allows them to do that by default).
- Turn off access to Contacts for individual applications. The following apps are listed there by default:

  ° Email and accounts
  ° Maps
  ° Photos
  ° Skype
  ° Twitter
  ° Voice Recorder
  ° Xbox

Privacy → Calendar

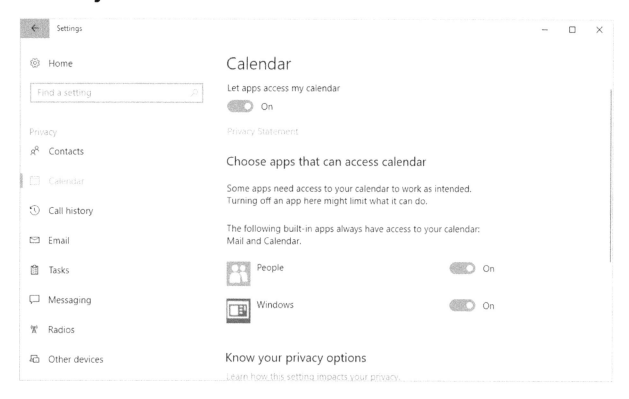

This page controls which applications may access calendar information. The Mail and Calendar application has access to calendar data even if this is turned off. The following options are provided:

- Let apps access my calendar. Determines whether calendar functionality is enabled.
- Turn access to Calendar data off for select applications. The following apps are listed by default:

  ° People
  ° Windows

Privacy → Call History

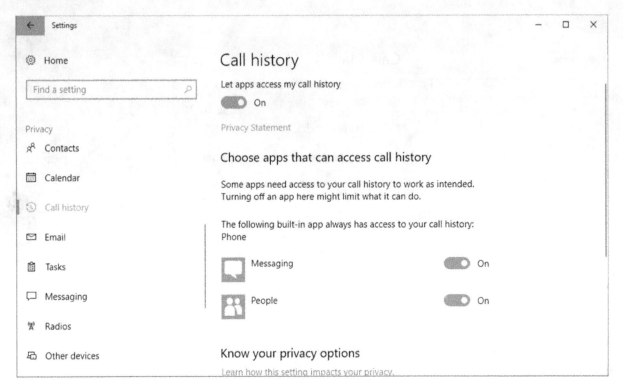

Control access to the Call History by applications on this page. The Phone application has access to the call history even if the feature is turned off.

- **Let apps access my call history.** This setting determines whether applications may access the call history on the device.
- Turn off access to the Call History for select applications. This works only if the setting is enabled. The following applications are configured for access automatically.

  ○ Messaging
  ○ People

- The following application has hardcoded access to the Call History

  ○ Phone

Privacy → Email

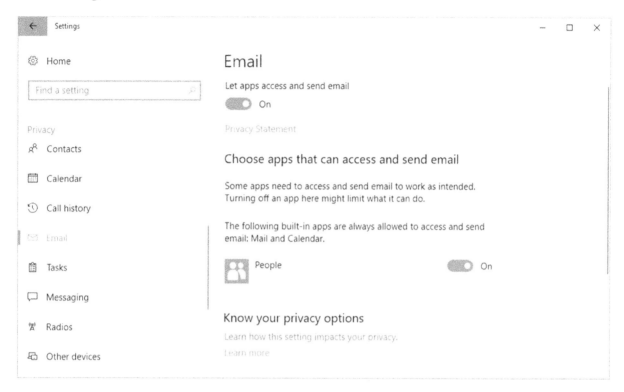

The page allows you to control if applications may access and send email. The Mail and Calendar application is allowed to send and access email regardless of setting. The following options are provided:

- **Let apps access and send email**. Apps need permission to access or transfer emails.
- Choose apps that can access and send email. This relies on the general setting to work. The following application is setup by to access and send email by default.

  ◦ People

- The following applications have hardcoded access that cannot be revoked:

  ◦ Mail and Calendar

Privacy → Tasks

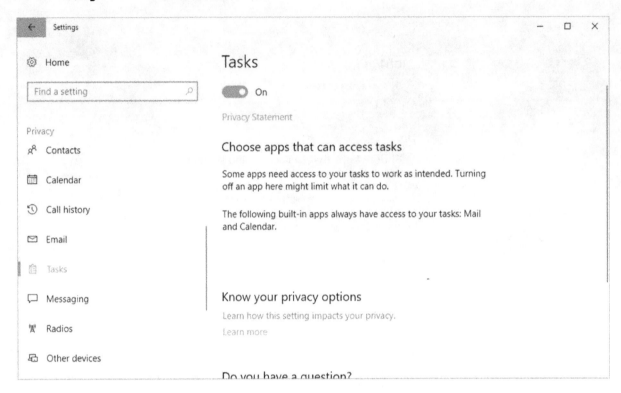

You may allow or deny Tasks access to applications. The Mail and Calendar application has access to Tasks regardless of setting. You can change the following preferences here:

- **Control Tasks access by applications for the whole device**.
- Control Tasks access for individual applications.
- The following applications have hardcoded access to Tasks; this cannot be turned off:

  ○ Mail and Calendar

Privacy → Messaging

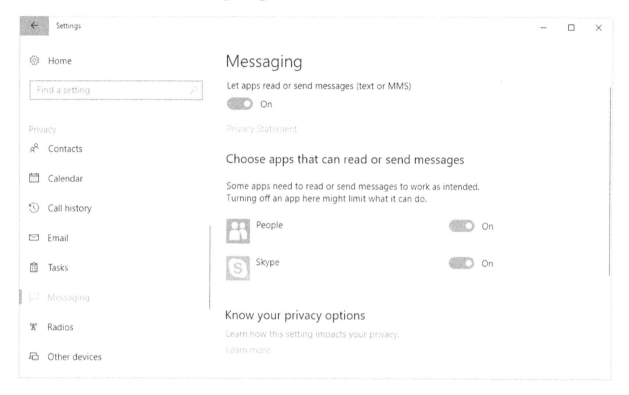

Here you may define if applications may read or send messages using text or MMS. The following options are listed:

- **Let apps read or send messages (text or MMS).** Turn the feature on or off completely.
- Choose which applications may read or send messages. The following apps are configured to do so by default:

    ◦ People
    ◦ Skype

Privacy → Radios

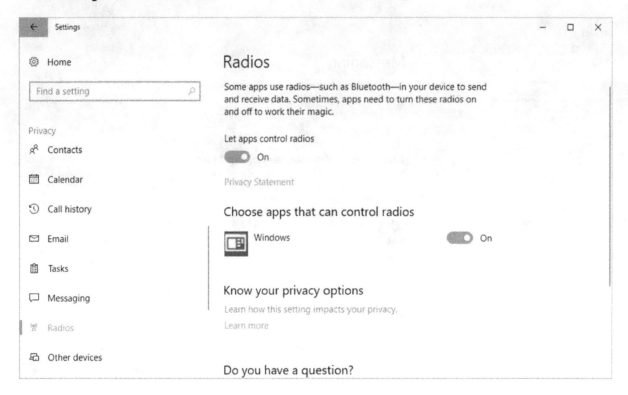

You can control radio use by applications, Bluetooth functionality for instance, on this page. This setting does not define whether applications may use radios, but whether they may control them. The following options are provided:

- **Select whether applications may control radios such as Bluetooth**. This allows them to turn them on or off, or make use of radios.
- Choose which applications may control radios. The following applications are set up to control radios by default:

  ° Windows

Privacy → Other devices

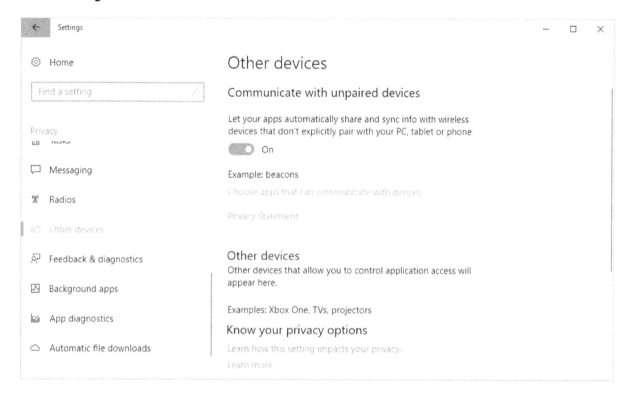

"Other devices" defines the sync behavior with other devices such as PCs, tablets or phones. This setting is for "other devices" that don't pair explicitly with the device already. The following options are provided:

- **Let your apps automatically share and sync info with wireless devices that don't explicitly pair with your PC, tablet or phone**.
- Select which apps may sync info or share automatically with wireless devices.
- Manage the list of other devices.

Privacy → Feedback & Diagnostics

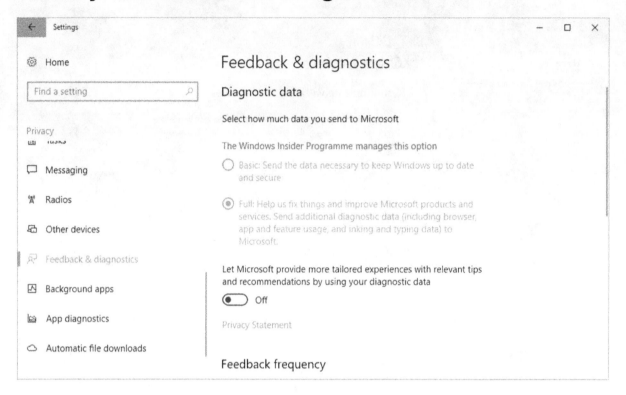

You control how much data is sent to Microsoft here. Also, if that data is used for tailored experiences, and the frequency that Windows displays feedback prompts. The following options are provided:

- **Select how much data you sent to Microsoft.** Switch between Full and Basic telemetry settings. This is one of the options displayed on the Privacy page during setup. For detailed information on Telemetry, check out the Telemetry chapter of this book.
- **Let Microsoft provide more tailored experiences with relevant tips and recommendations by using your diagnostic data**. Enable or disable the tailored experiences functionality. This was also part of the Privacy page during setup.
- Control the feedback frequency (default automatic), or turn the feature off completely.

Privacy → Background apps

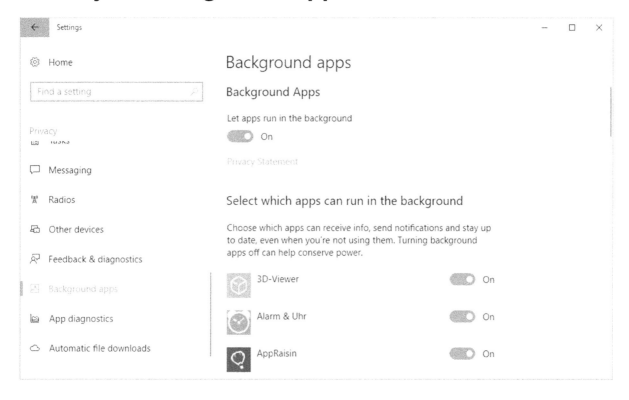

You may allow or deny applications to run in the background using this setting. The following options are provided:

- **Turn background application functionality on or off for all applications.**
- Choose which applications may run in the background. This is only active if the general setting is turned on. The following applications are set up to run in the background by default:

  - 3D Viewer
  - Alarms & Clock
  - Calculator
  - Camera
  - Connect
  - Feedback Hub
  - Get Help
  - Get Office
  - Groove Music
  - Mail
  - Maps

- Messaging
- Microsoft Edge
- Microsoft Solitaire Collection
- Minecraft: Windows 10 Editions
- Movies & TV
- News
- OneNote
- Paid Wi-Fi & Cellular
- Paint 3D
- People
- Photos
- Settings
- Skype
- Sticky Notes
- Store
- Tips
- Twitter
- Voice Recorder
- Weather
- Windows Defender Security Center
- Xbox

Privacy → App diagnostics

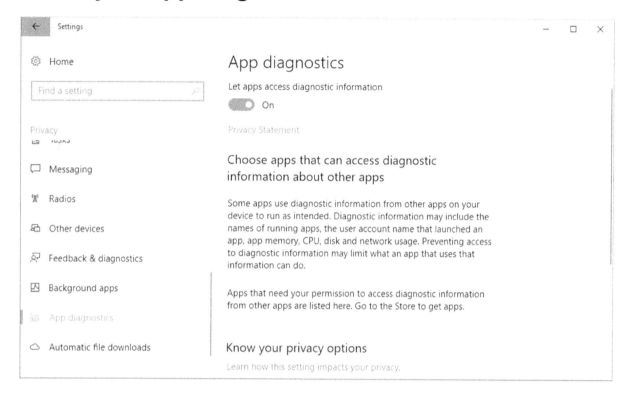

The last privacy setting lists options to control whether applications may access diagnostic data.

Diagnostic data may include the names of running applications, the user account that launched an app, app memory information, CPU, disk and network usage.

The following options are provided:

- **Choose whether apps may use diagnostic data on the machine**.
- Select which individual apps may access diagnostic data.

Privacy → Automatic file downloads

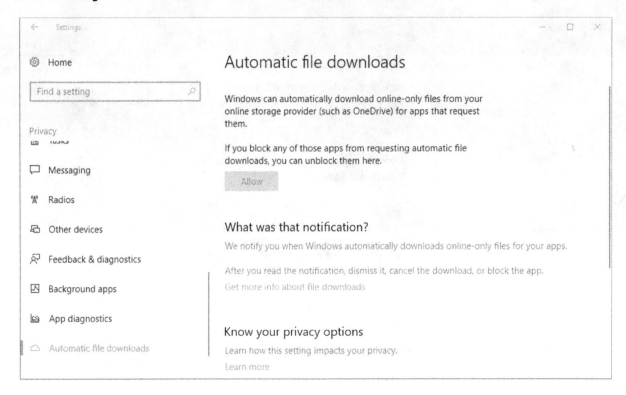

Windows 10 may download files automatically from online storage providers such as OneDrive if the files are available only online.

The setting lets you unblock applications that you blocked from downloading files automatically.

Windows 10 notifies you when apps want to download files automatically, and you may allow it, dismiss the message, cancel the downloading or block the application from

QUICK OVERVIEW: DIFFERENCES BETWEEN WINDOWS 10 EDITIONS

The Windows 10 operating system is offered in multiple editions. These can be divided into retail, organizational and special editions.

Retail: Windows 10 Home and Windows 10 Pro

Organizational: Windows 10 Enterprise, Windows 10 Enterprise LTSC, Windows 10 Education, Windows 10 Pro Education, Windows 10 Mobile Enterprise

Special: Windows 10 Mobile, Windows 10 IoT, Windows 10 S, Windows 10 Team, Windows 10 Pro for Workstations

Consumers may select between Windows 10 Home and Pro. The core difference from a privacy perspective is that Home does not ship with the Group Policy Editor. This makes it more difficult to apply certain settings on the system.

Windows 10 Pro includes business related features such as Remote Desktop, creating and joining domains, Trusted Boot, or Enterprise Mode Internet Explorer on top of that, and is more expensive than the Home edition of the operating system.

There are core differences between Retail and Organizational editions. Organizational editions support the "Security" Telemetry level which Home and Pro editions do not support. They also support the recently announced Window Analytics setting.

The default Telemetry level is Full on all editions of Windows 10 though.

Note: The next chapter gives you an overview of Telemetry; it offers detailed information on what Telemetry is, and how the different Telemetry levels differ from each other (based on information that Microsoft provided in the past).

Organizational editions of Windows 10 give you the best control over privacy related features.

If you run Windows 10 already, you can find out which version you have by tapping on the Windows-key, typing winver, and hitting the Enter-key.

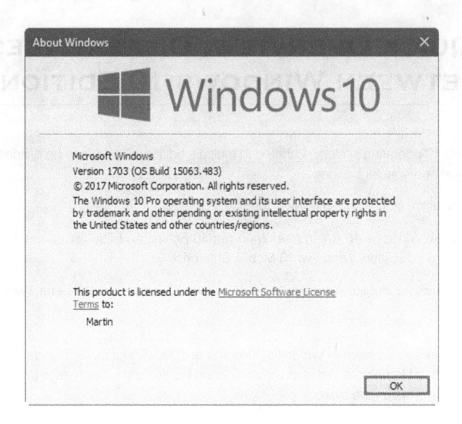

The window that opens lists the version and build of the operating system, and the edition.

Windows 10 Home systems can be upgraded to Windows 10 Pro.

Important information about tools used in this guide

To start the Group Policy Editor:

1. Tap on the Windows-key, type gpedit.msc, and hit the Enter-key. Note that the Group Policy Editor is only available in professional versions of Windows (basically, not in Home).

To load the Windows Registry Editor:

1. Tap on the Windows-key, type regedit.exe, and hit the Enter-key.
2. Confirm the UAC prompt.

Adding keys to the Registry:

If a Registry path is listed, it can happen sometimes that a key does not exist. You may create it with a right-click on its parent key in the Registry Editor, and selecting New > Key from the menu.

To load the Settings application:

1. Use the keyboard shortcut Windows-I.

To load an administrative command prompt:

1. Tap on the Windows-key, type cmd.exe, hold down the Shift-key and the Ctrl-key, and hit the Enter-key while the two keys are held down.

To load an elevated PowerShell prompt:

1. Tap on the Windows-key, type powershell, hold down the Shift-key and the Ctrl-key, and hit the Enter-key.

Telemetry

Windows as a Service is a fundamental change to Microsoft's previous system of planning, developing and releasing operating systems.

Microsoft released new Windows versions every few years in the past; Windows 7 in 2009 and Windows 8 in 2012 for instance, but that changed with the release of Windows 10 in the year 2015.

Microsoft realized that creating and deploying large Windows updates was a substantial effort in the past as it took three years of development to release a new version of Windows.

Windows as a Service changes the old release model by pushing out frequent updates – so called Feature Updates – instead. Main benefits of the new strategy are that development requires less resources, that it is less time consuming, and that new features and changes are pushed out faster to the existing customer base.

The company plans to release two feature updates per year for Windows 10; a much faster pace when compared to the classic release model.

The following feature updates have been released so far:

- July 29, 2015 – Windows 10 RTM (Release to Manufacturing)
- November 12, 2015 – Windows 10 November Update, version 1511
- August 2, 2016 – Windows 10 Anniversary Update, version 1607
- April 5, 2017 – The Windows 10 Creators Update, version 1703
- October 17, 2017 -- The Windows 10 Fall Creators Update, version 1709

Telemetry is not a new concept; Microsoft did collect Telemetry data in previous versions of the company's Windows operating system as well, for instance to check whether the installation of Windows updates was successful, or to gather reliability information through the CEIP (Windows Customer Experience Improvement Program).

Windows as a Service makes Telemetry data more important however in Windows 10. The shorter release cycle is one core reason for that, as the next Windows 10 feature update is just six months away and not three years anymore.

Microsoft has to prioritize decision making and development, and Telemetry data helps the company in that decision-making process.

What is Telemetry

Microsoft defines Telemetry in the following ways:

> *Windows telemetry is vital technical data from Windows devices about the device and how Windows and related software are performing.*[11]

> *Telemetry is system data that is uploaded by the Connected User Experience and Telemetry component. The telemetry data is used to keep Windows devices secure, and to help Microsoft improve the quality of Windows and Microsoft services. It is used to provide a service to the user as part of Windows.*

According to Microsoft, Telemetry is used for

- Keeping Windows up to date.
- Keeping Windows secure, reliable and performant.
- Improving Windows through the use of aggregate Windows use data.
- Personalizing the Windows engagement surface.
- Better understanding how customers use (or don't) use operating system features and services.

Specific examples of Windows telemetry data that Microsoft provides include:

- The type of hardware that is being used.
- The applications that are installed, and usage information.
- Device driver reliability information.
- Monitoring the scalability of the Cortana cloud service.
- How users customize the Windows Start Menu.

Microsoft states that it uses Telemetry data to identify security and reliability issues in Windows 10, to analyze problems, to improve the quality of Windows, and for making future development decisions.

It needs to be noted that Telemetry is not a Windows-specific feature. Many companies, including Google, Mozilla or Tesla, collect Telemetry data.

Microsoft differentiates between Telemetry and functional data. Telemetry is what Microsoft collects, as described above.

> *Operational data, such as telemetry, enables us to provide you with core operating system services, such as Windows Update, and gives every enterprise customer a voice in helping shape future versions of Windows. We can provide quick responses to your feedback and your feedback helps us define new features and improve quality.*[12]

---

[11] https://docs.microsoft.com/en-us/windows/configuration/configure-windows-telemetry-in-your-organization

[12] https://www.microsoft.com/en-us/trustcenter/Privacy/windows-telemetry-privacy-and-trust.aspx

Functional data on the other hand is exchanged by Windows apps and components to provide users with information or functionality they require or provide. A basic example is the use of location data to look up weather information or display local news.

> *Functional data is created and used by specific applications or components of Windows, such as Cortana and Bing, and gives you customized experiences that help increase your productivity and enjoyment of your Windows devices.[13]*

While Telemetry cannot be turned off completely, depending on the edition that is used it is either set to Security or Basic at a minimum, functional data can be blocked completely.

The blocking of functional data restricts some features of the Windows 10 operating system and applications that require the data to function properly.

Important

Telemetry only applies to Windows, Windows Server, and System Center components, and apps that use Connected User Experience or Telemetry components.

There are four Telemetry levels as of Windows 10 version 1709 which are described in detail on the next pages.

The lowest Telemetry level supported through Management Policies is Security, and only available in Enterprise editions of Windows 10 (see Telemetry Levels below for detailed information on editions).

The lowest Telemetry level supported through the Settings UI is Basic.

All Telemetry data is encrypted using SSL when it is transferred to the Microsoft Data Management Service. Microsoft's implementation uses certificate pinning as well.

Telemetry data is uploaded on a schedule that takes into account event priority, battery use, and network costs.

> *With Windows 10, data is uploaded on a schedule that is sensitive to event priority, battery use, and network cost. Real-time events, such as Windows Defender Advanced Threat Protection, are always sent immediately.*

> *Normal events are not uploaded on metered networks, unless you are on a metered server connection. On a free network, normal events can be uploaded every 4 hours if on battery, or every 15 minutes if on A/C power. Diagnostic and crash data are only uploaded on A/C power and free networks.[14]*

---

[13] https://www.microsoft.com/en-us/trustcenter/Privacy/windows-telemetry-privacy-and-trust.aspx

[14] https://docs.microsoft.com/en-us/windows/configuration/configure-windows-telemetry-in-your-organization

How does Windows 10 collect Telemetry data?

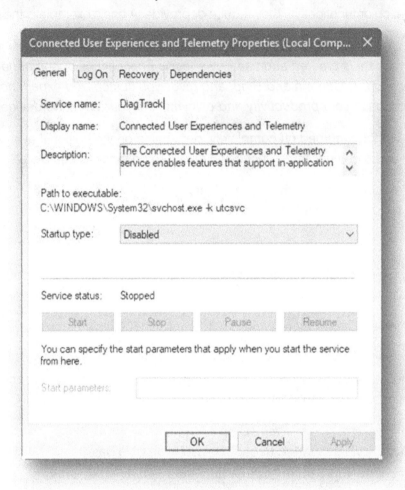

All Windows 10 editions come with the Connected User Experiences and Telemetry service. This service is run by the Connected User Experience and Telemetry component.

The service's name is Connected User Experiences and Telemetry, its display name is DiagTrack, and its service name is utcsvc.

The service's description reads:

> *The Connected User Experiences and Telemetry service enables features that support in-application and connected user experiences.*

> *Additionally, this service manages the event driven collection and transmission of diagnostic and usage information (used to improve the experience and quality of the Windows Platform) when the diagnostics and usage privacy option settings are enabled under Feedback and Diagnostics.*

Telemetry data is stored in the hidden system folder %ProgramData%\Microsoft\Diagnosis

Note that the data is encrypted, and that permissions make it difficult to access these folders.

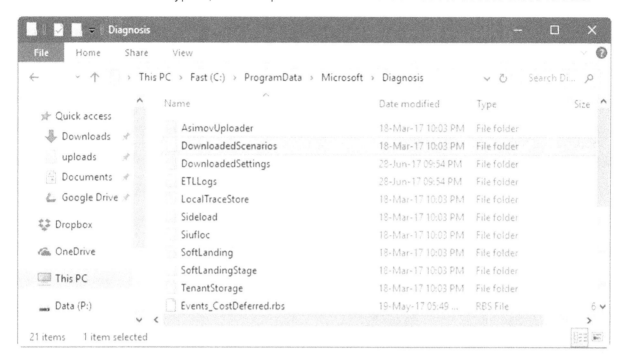

Windows 10 connects to the Telemetry endpoints, listed in the following chapter, when it is time to transfer data to Microsoft.

The Telemetry client connects to settings-win.data.microsoft.com to download a settings file and provide a device ID and other basic information.

The settings file is parsed, and then used to connect to v10.vortex-win.data.microsoft.com, the Microsoft Data Management Service to upload the Telemetry data.

Telemetry levels Overview

Windows 10 supports the four Telemetry levels: Security, Basic, Enhanced and Full. Only two of those levels, Basic and Full, can be set in the Settings application by users of the operating system.

One level, Security, is only available in Windows 10 Enterprise, Windows 10 Server, and Education .

The fourth level, Enhanced, is available in all editions, but can only be set using the Group Policy or by making changes to the Windows Registry.

Security – Information required to help keep Windows secure. It collects data that is required to keep Windows secure and protected with the latest security updates. Not an option under Settings.

- applies to: Windows Server 2016, Windows 10 Enterprise, Windows 10 Education, Windows 10 Mobile Enterprise, and Windows IoT Core editions

Basic – Basic includes all Security data, and data that Microsoft calls "critical for understanding the device and its configuration".

- applies to: all editions of Windows 10. Minimum setting for all editions that are not listed under Security above.

Enhanced – A Telemetry level of Enhanced includes all data that is sent on the Basic level, plus additional data on how apps, Windows, Windows Server, or System Center are used, and how they perform. Not an option under Settings, can only be set using policies or the Registry.

- applies to: all editions of Windows 10.

Full – The Full level includes all basic and security data sets. Additionally,

- applies to: all editions of Windows 10.
- Default on: Windows 10 Insider Preview systems, on Windows 10 Pro and Home. Windows 10 Enterprise, Windows 10 Education, Windows 10 Server.

Security

Note: Organizations should not use the Security telemetry level if they rely on Windows Update for updates according to Microsoft. The main reason Microsoft gives for that is that Windows Update information is not gathered on this level, and that means that information about update failures is not submitted. Microsoft uses the data to repair issues that cause updates to fail, and to improve the quality of updates.

Organizations may want to use this Telemetry level for computer systems without Internet connectivity, as this stops the gathering of data that would not be transferred anyway.

Also, the level is suitable for machines which should not communicate with the outside world, and for environments where communication with outside servers needs to be kept to a minimum.

Data gathered on this level

Security is the lowest Telemetry level. It is only available in Enterprise-editions of Windows 10 (see full compatibility list in the previous chapter).

Connected User Experience and Telemetry component settings

If general telemetry data has been gathered and is queued, it is sent to Microsoft. Along with this telemetry data, the Connected User Experience and Telemetry component may download a configuration settings file from Microsoft's servers.

This file is used to configure the Connected User Experience and Telemetry component itself.

The data gathered by the client for this request includes OS information, device id (used to identify what specific device is requesting settings) and device class (for example, whether the device is server or desktop).

Malicious Software Removal Tool (MSRT)

The MSRT infection report contains information, including device info and IP address.

Note: MSRT infection reports can be turned off. See Deploy Windows Malicious Software Removal Tool in an Enterprise environment for information: https://support.microsoft.com/en-us/help/891716/deploy-windows-malicious-software-removal-tool-in-an-enterprise-environment

Windows Defender / Endpoint Protection

Windows Defender and System Center Endpoint Protection requires some information to function, including: anti-malware signatures, diagnostic information, User Account Control settings, Unified Extensible Firmware Interface (UEFI) settings, and IP address.

Note: The reporting can be turned off: https://docs.microsoft.com/en-us/windows/configuration/manage-connections-from-windows-operating-system-components-to-microsoft-services#bkmk-defender

Microsoft states that no user content is gathered at this level. User content includes user files or communication. Steps are taken to avoid the gathering of user or company identifying information such as email addresses, names, or account IDs.

It may happen unintentionally however through MSRT as reports may contain personal information.

MSRT information may unintentionally contain personal information. For instance, some malware may create entries in a computer's registry that include information such as a username, causing it to be gathered. MSRT reporting is optional and can be turned off at any time.

Basic

Basic is one of the two Telemetry levels that Microsoft lists during setup and in the Windows 10 Settings application.

It is not the default level however, and must be set by users or administrators.

Data gathered on this level

Basic is the second-lowest Telemetry level. It includes all data that is collected on the Security level (see description above), plus additional data.

This additional data can be divided into device information, quality related information, and inventory related information.

Basic Device Data

- Internet Explorer version
- Device attributes such as camera resolution and display type.
- Battery attributes.
- Networking attributes such as the number of network adapters or IMEI number.
- Processor and memory attributes such as number of cores, memory size, or architecture.
- Storage attributes such as the number of hard drives, type of drives, and size.
- Operating system attributes such as the Windows edition and virtualization state.
- Virtualization attributes, such as guest operating system or SLAT support.

Connected User Experience and Telemetry component quality metrics

This includes information on how Telemetry and Connected User Experience components function and work. Information that is transferred includes data on uploaded and dropped events, and the last upload time.

Quality related information

Data that provides Microsoft with information on how a device and Windows performs.

Data includes the number of crashes and hangs, application state change details such as how much memory and processor time were used, and characteristics of a Connected Standby device.

Compatibility data

- List of installed applications including application names, publisher information, versions, as well as Internet Explorer add-ons.

- Data on how apps are used, how long individual apps are open, have focus, and when apps are started.
- System data that Microsoft uses to determine whether a device meets the minimum requirements to update to the next version of Windows. Also includes memory, as well as information on the processor and BIOS.
- List of accessory devices such as printers or external hard drives. Also, compatibility information to determine if they are compatible with the next version of Windows.
- Data on installed drivers, including whether these are compatible with the next version of Windows.

Microsoft Store

This set of data includes information on how Microsoft Store performs on the device.

Information includes the number of app downloads, installations and updates.

Also, Microsoft Store launches, page views, suspend and resume operations, and license obtaining.

Enhanced

The Enhanced Telemetry level can only be set using policies or the Registry. See the next chapter – Configuring Telemetry on Windows 10 – for instructions on changing the Telemetry level.

This level helps to improve the user experience with the operating system and apps.

Data from this level can be abstracted into patterns and trends that can help Microsoft determine future improvements.

Data gathered on this level

The enhanced level includes all data from the Security and Basic level.

- Operating system events including networking, Hyper-V, Cortana, storage, file system.
- Operating system app events that result from Microsoft applications and management tools download from Store, or that came pre-installed with the operating system (such as Microsoft Edge, Mail, or Photos).
- Device specific events such as Surface Hub or Microsoft HoloLens data (which is not part on regular computer systems).
- A selection of crash dump types.

Full

Full data includes all data that is collected on the Security, Basic and Enhanced level, plus additional information listed below.

It is the default level on all non-Enterprise, Education and Server operating system editions of Windows 10.

Data gathered on this level

- ° App usage, input reaction, or how long each app runs.
- ° Browser usage, including browsing history and search terms.
- ° Samples (small according to Microsoft) of inking and typing support. Microsoft notes that the data is processed to remove identifiable information such as email addresses, names, or numeric values.
- ° Enhanced error reporting like the memory state of the device, when system or app crashes occurred.
- ° Status and logging information about the health of the operating system.
- ° Additional device data, connectivity information, and configuration data beyond that what is already collected on the Basic level.

Endpoints for Telemetry Services

Service	Endpoint
Connected User Experience and Telemetry component	v10.vortex-win.data.microsoft.com settings-win.data.microsoft.com
Windows Error Reporting	watson.telemetry.microsoft.com
Online Crash Analysis	oca.telemetry.microsoft.com
OneDrive app for Windows 10	vortex.data.microsoft.com/collect/v1

Configuring Windows 10 Telemetry settings

Windows 10 users and administrators have three options when it comes to setting the Telemetry level (switching to a level that is not the default).

The Settings application limits the levels to Basic and Full. You can set the Security and Enhanced levels only through other means, for instance by using the Group Policy or editing the Registry.

Note that you can set the Security level on non-Enterprise version through the Registry or Group Policy, but that the setting is changed to Basic automatically in that case.

Option 1: Settings application

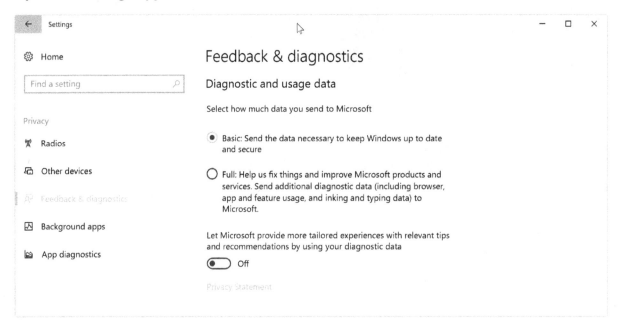

1. Use the keyboard shortcut Windows-I to open the Settings application.
2. Navigate to Privacy > Feedback & Diagnostics
3. Locate the "Select how much data you send to Microsoft" section.
4. You have the option to switch between Basic and Full levels there.

Option 2: Group Policy

1. Tap on the Windows-key, type gpedit.msc, and hit the Enter-key on the keyboard.
2. Use the folder structure on the left to navigate to Computer Configuration > Administrative Templates > Windows Components > Data Collection and Feedback
3. Double-click on "Allow Telemetry".
4. Set the policy to Enabled.

5. Select one of the available levels (Security, Basic, Enhanced, Full).

   1. Note that Security applies only to Enterprise, EDU and IoT. While you may set the level on other editions of Windows 10, this is then handled like Basic automatically. In other words, the lowest level you can set on Home and Pro editions of Windows 10 is Basic.

Option 3: Windows Registry

1. Tap on the Windows-key, type regedit.exe, and hit the Enter-key on the keyboard.
2. Navigate to the following key: HKEY_LOCAL_MACHINE\Software\Microsoft\Windows\CurrentVersion\Policies\DataCollection
3. Right-click on DataCollection, and select New > Dword (32-bit) Value.
4. Name it AllowTelemetry.
5. Double-click on the new value AllowTelemetry, and set its value according to the table below. Again, Security is automatically changed to Basic on Home and Pro editions of Windows 10.
6. Restart the PC afterwards.

Level	Data gathered	Value
Security	Security data only.	0
Basic	Security data, and basic system and quality data.	1
Enhanced	Security data, basic system and quality data, and enhanced insights and advanced reliability data.	2
Full	Security data, basic system and quality data, enhanced insights and advanced reliability data, and full diagnostics data.	3

Business and Enterprise options

Options to turn off Telemetry are also provided in System Center 2016 by using the System Center UI Console settings workspace.

Another option is provided by MDM. You may use the Policy Configuration Service Provider (CSP) to apply the AllowTelemetry MDM policy.

Manage Connections from Windows components to Microsoft

Windows 10 and Windows 10 Server administrators and users may control the handling of Telemetry and other connections that Windows and apps make to Microsoft individually as well.

The following chapters highlight these options. Most apply to all editions of Windows 10.

It needs to be noted that some options, such as MDM policy or Group Policy, are not available for all versions of Windows 10.

Please note that it is recommended to go through the list and decide for each setting individually how you want to configure it.

Some may be required for functionality. If you disable location for all apps, you cannot use certain features that require location. The same is true for other features, so that the decision should be based on your use of the operating system, and what you feel comfortable with.

SETTINGS FOR WINDOWS 10

Some programs and services ship with their own Telemetry data settings which you need to disable manually if you don't want the data to be sent to Microsoft. I have listed those in other chapters in this guide.

This is true for instance for the Messenger application.

Certificate Trust Lists

A predefined list of items, for instance of certificate hashes or file names, that are signed. Windows will download an updated certificate trust list when it is updated.

You can turn off the automatic downloading of the updated list by turning off automatic root updates.

Note: Web connectivity issues may occur when you disable the root certificate updating.

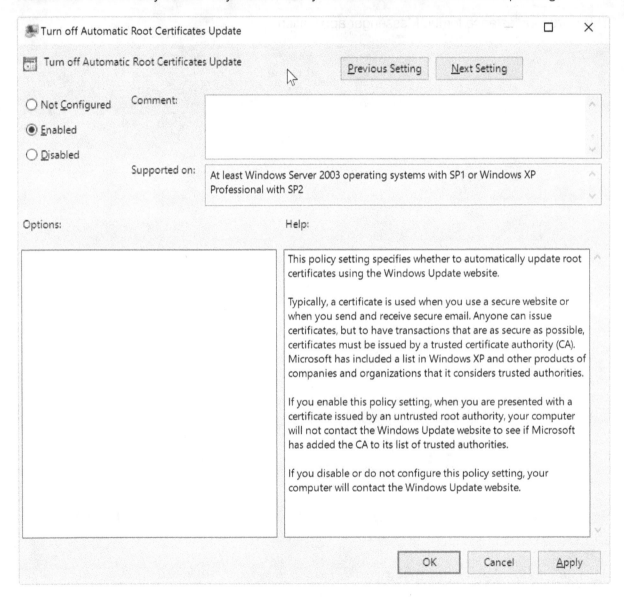

1. Open the Group Policy Editor, and go to Computer Configuration > Administrative Templates > System > Internet Communication Management > Internet Communication Settings > Turn

off Automatic Root Certificates Update. Set this to enabled to disable the automatic updating of Root Certificates

2. If you prefer the Windows Registry instead, do the following:

    1. Open the Windows Registry Editor, and go to HKEY_LOCAL_MACHINE\SOFTWARE\ Policies\Microsoft\SystemCertificates\AuthRoot
    2. If a key does not exist, right-click on the parent key, and select New > Key to create it.
    3. Right-click on AuthRoot, and select New > Dword (32-bit) Value.
    4. Name it DisableRootAutoUpdate.
    5. Double-click on the new value, and set its value to 1.

3. While still in the Group Policy Editor, go to Computer Configuration > Windows Settings > Security Settings > Public Key Policies

    1. Select Certificate Path Validation Settings by double-clicking on it.
    2. On the Network Retrieval tab, select Define these policy settings.
    3. Uncheck the Automatically update certificates in the Microsoft Root Certificate Program (recommended)

Cortana and Search

Cortana is a digital agent that is part of the Windows 10 operating system. Microsoft linked Cortana to search, as it may be used to run web searches for the user.

Cortana is configured to make life easier for the user. The digital agent may be used to keep track of dates or events, track pages, your favorite sports team or flights, to create and manage lists, and to send emails or texts.

Cortana returns web search results powered by Bing by default for queries. This was limited to search term suggestions in older versions of Windows 10, but has since then been expanded by Microsoft.

Web search displays the Bing results page on the desktop when you run searches in the Fall Creators Update.

Windows users may disable Cortana, but may still use Windows Search to find local files, settings and information when they do so.

Allow Cortana

This policy determines whether Cortana is allowed on the device. Note that users may still use Windows Search to find files, settings and other information on the device when they disable Cortana on the machine.

Group Policy

Computer Configuration > Administrative Templates > Windows Components > Search > Allow Cortana

- Enabled – Same as not configured. Cortana is allowed on the device.
- Disabled – Cortana is disabled.

Windows Registry

1. Go to HKEY_LOCAL_MACHINE\SOFTWARE\Microsoft\PolicyManager\current\device\ Experience
2. If Experience does not exist, right-click on device and select New > Key. Name the key Experience.
3. Right-click on Experience, and select New Dword (32-bit) Value.

    1. Set its value to 0 to disallow Cortana.
    2. Set its value to 1 to allow Cortana.

Alternatively

1. Go to HKEY_LOCAL_MACHINE\SOFTWARE\Policies\Microsoft\Windows\Windows Search
2. Create Dword (32-bit) Value Allow Cortana

    1. Set its value to 0 to disallow Cortana
    2. Set its value 1 or delete the preference to allow Cortana.

3. Additionally, on 64-bit versions of Windows:

    1. Go to HKEY_LOCAL_MACHINE\SOFTWARE\WOW6432Node\Policies\Microsoft\Windows\Windows Search\
    2. Right-click on Windows Search, select New > Dword (32-bit) Value.
    3. Name it AllowCortana

        1. Set its value to 0 to disallow Cortana
        2. Set its value to 1 to allow Cortana

Allow Search and Cortana to use location

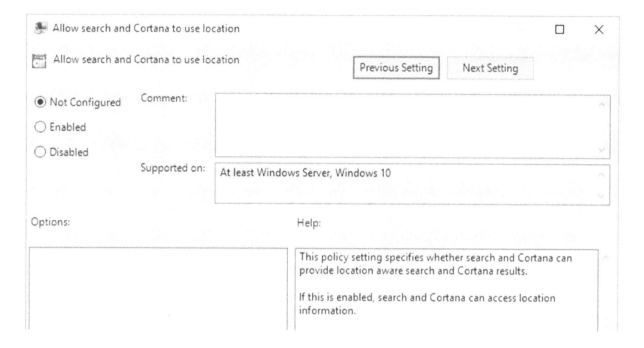

This policy defines whether Windows Search and Cortana can use the device's location to deliver location aware search results.

Group Policy

Computer Configuration > Administrative Templates > Windows Components > Search > Allow search and Cortana to use location

- Enabled – Cortana and Search are allowed to access location information, and will use the data for location aware search results.
- Disabled – Cortana and Search may not use location information.

Windows Registry

Allow search and Cortana to use location

Key: HKEY_LOCAL_MACHINE\SOFTWARE\Policies\Microsoft\Windows\Windows Search

Name: AllowSearchToUseLocation

Type: Dword

- Set its value to 0 to disallow search to use the location.
- Set the value to 1 or delete the Dword value to allow search to use the location.

Do not allow web search

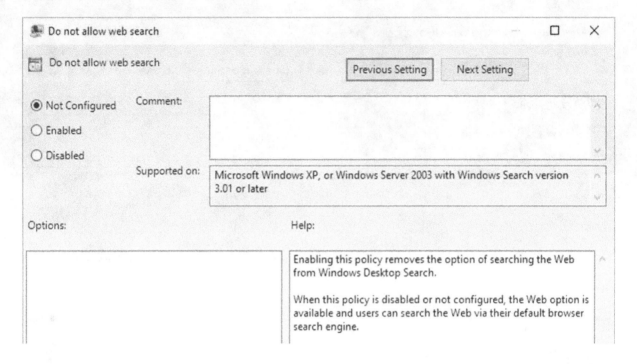

This policy defines whether Windows Desktop Search may search the Web when you type in the searcb box, and return Web results.

Group Policy

Computer Configuration > Administrative Templates > Windows Components > Search > Do not allow web search

- Enabled – If you enable the policy, Web Search options are not available.
- Disabled – Same as not configured. The option to search the web is available, and users can search the Web using the default search engine.

Windows Registry

Key: HKEY_LOCAL_MACHINE\SOFTWARE\Policies\Microsoft\Windows\Windows Search

Name: DisableWebSearch

Type: Dword

- Set its value to 1 to disable web searching.
- Set its value to 0 to enable web searching, or delete the value.

Don't search the web or display web results in Search

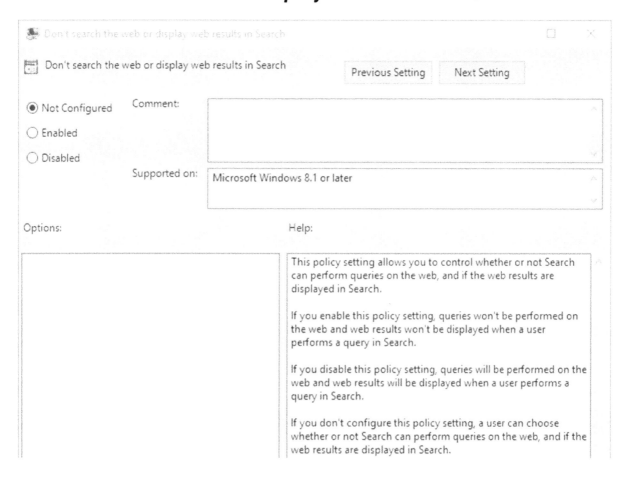

This policy allows you to control whether Search may run web search queries, and whether web results are displayed by Windows Search.

Group Policy

Computer Configuration > Administrative Templates > Windows Components > Search > Don't search the web or display web results in Search

- Enabled – If you enable the policy, Windows Search won't run or return web queries.
- Disabled – Windows Search will search the Web, and web results are displayed in Search.
- Not Configured – Users are in control and may configure Search to include Web results, or block Search from doing so.

Windows Registry:

Key: HKEY_LOCAL_MACHINE\SOFTWARE\Policies\Microsoft\Windows\Windows Search

Name: ConnectedSearchUseWeb

Type: Dword

- Set its value to 0 to disable searching the web or displaying web results.
- Set its value to 1 or delete the preference to allow web searching

Don't search the web or display web results in Search over metered connections

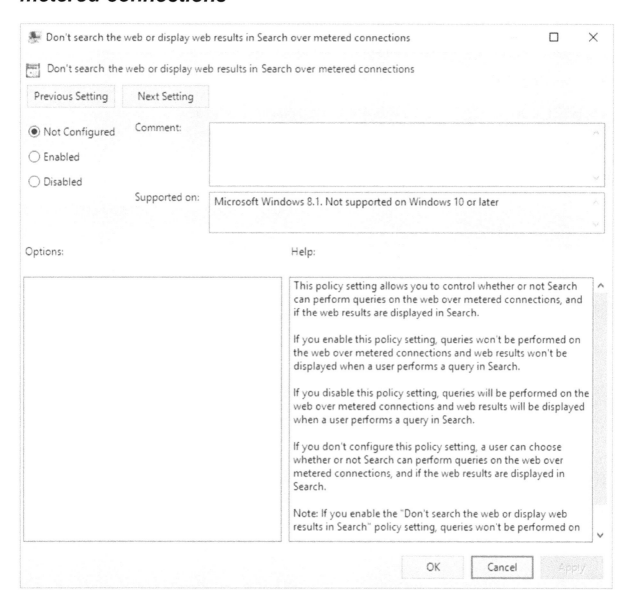

This is essentially the same as the policy above, but it applies only to metered connections. If you enable the "Don't search the web or display web results in Search" policy, queries won't be performed regardless of how you configure this policy.

Group Policy

Computer Configuration > Administrative Templates > Windows Components > Search > Don't search the web or display web results in Search over metered connections

- Enabled – If you enable this policy, Search won't run web searches or display them in the Search results if the PC is a metered connection is used.
- Disabled – Web searches are run over metered connections, and results are displayed by Search.
- Not Configured – Users are in control, and may enable or disable the feature.

Windows Registry

Key: HKEY_LOCAL_MACHINE\SOFTWARE\Policies\Microsoft\Windows\Windows Search

Name: ConnectedSearchUseWebOverMeteredConnections

Type: Dword

- Set its value to 0 to disable the feature. Web Search is enabled over metered connections.
- Set its value to 1 to enable it.

Set what information is shared in Search

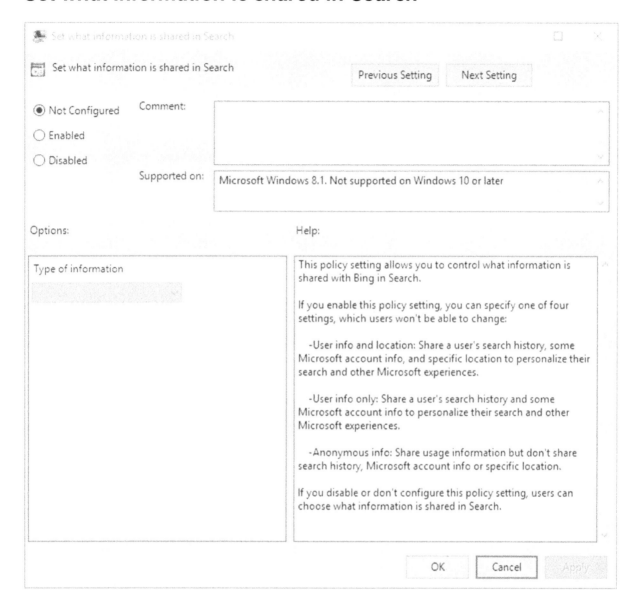

This policy defines which information is shared with Bing when web searches are run. Available options include sharing user information and location, user information only, or anonymous information.

Group Policy

Computer Configuration > Administrative Templates > Windows Components > Search > Set what information Is shared in Search

- Enabled – If you enable this setting, you may select one of the following data sets when it comes to sharing with Bing:

  - User info and location – Shares both information on the user, the search history, and specific location information to personalize search and "other Microsoft experiences".
  - User info only – This shares user information, but no location information.
  - Anonymous info – Shares usage information, but no Microsoft Account, search history, or location data.

- Disabled -- Same as not configured. Users may choose what is shared in Search.

Windows Registry

Key: HKEY_LOCAL_MACHINE\SOFTWARE\Policies\Microsoft\Windows\Windows Search

Name: ConnectedSearchPrivacy

Type: Dword

- A value of 1 means User info and location is shared.
- A value of 2 means only user info is shared.
- A value of 3 means only anonymous info is shared.

Set the SafeSearch setting for Search

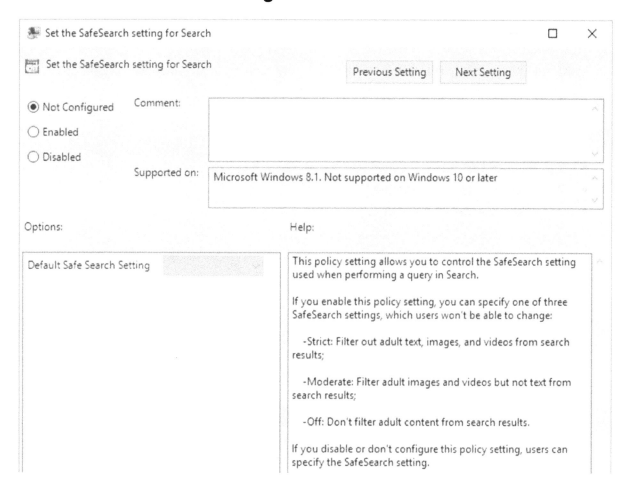

SafeSearch determines whether a filter is being used to filter out inappropriate content. This is the same filter that is available on Bing directly when you run searches using the search engine.

Options include setting the search filter to strict, moderate or off. Users are allowed to specify the filter if the policy is not configured.

Group Policy

Computer Configuration > Administrative Templates > Windows Components > Search > Set the SafeSearch setting for Search

- Enabled – If you enable the policy, you may set the SafeSearch filter to the following values:
    - ° Strict – Filters out adult text, images, and videos from search results.
    - ° Moderate – Filters adult images and videos only.
    - ° Off – Does not filter.

- Disabled – Same as not. Configured. Search is enabled, and users may configure the filter level.

Windows Registry

Key: HKEY_LOCAL_MACHINE\SOFTWARE\Policies\Microsoft\Windows\Windows Search

Name: ConnectedSearchSafeSearch

Type: Dword

- 1 -- Value of 1 means strict filtering.
- 2 -- Value of 2 means moderate filtering.
- 3 -- Value of 3 means no filtering.

Cortana and Search MDM Policies

The following Cortana MDM policies are available in the Policy CSP

- Experience/AllowCortana – Select whether to allow or disallow Cortana on Windows 10 machines.
- Search/AllowSearchToUseLocation – Choose whether Cortana or Search may use location data to provide location-aware search results
- Linguistic Data Collection can be disabled in Settings > Privacy. Microsoft uses data collected by the Enhanced and Full Telemetry levels to improve features such as spellchecking, suggestions, or dictionaries.
- Windows Defender Cloud-based Protection and Automatic Sample Submission can be turned off in Settings > Update & Security > Windows Defender.
- Windows Update Telemetry can only be turned off if you disable Windows Updates, or if you set the device to be managed by an on premises update server such as WSUS (Windows Server Update Services), or System Center Configuration Manager.
- You can disable the infection reporting of the Microsoft Removal Tool as well by adding the following Registry key to the Windows 10 system:

    ° HKEY_LOCAL_MACHINE\SOFTWARE\Policies\Microsoft\MRT
    ° Dword (32-bit) Name: DontReportInfectionInformation
    ° Value data: 1

Date & Time

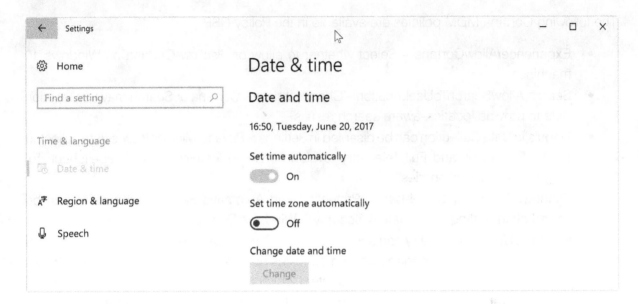

You can configure Windows so that it won't set the time automatically. You may turn off the feature in the Settings application:

1. Open the Settings application with Windows-I.
2. Go to Time & language > Date & Time
3. Toggle Set Time Automatically.
4. Set Time Zone automatically to off.

Note that if you do, you may need to set the time manually. This is the case for instance you need to adjust the time forward or backward one hour for daylight saving time. Windows handles this for you automatically if you let it sync the time.

If you disable set time zone automatically, Windows won't adjust the time automatically when you travel to locations that are in a different time zone.

Note that some Windows features – such as Windows Update – rely on accurate date and time information. They may not work properly if date and time are inaccurate.

You may also disable the syncing of time using the Registry

Open the Windows Registry Editor.

1. Go to HKEY_LOCAL_MACHINE\SYSTEM\CurrentControlSet\Services\W32Time\Parameters\
2. Right-click on Parameters, and select New > String Value
3. Set the value to NoSync.

Then do either of the following:

1. Go to
    HKEY_LOCAL_MACHINE\SOFTWARE\Policies\Microsoft\W32time\TimeProviders\NtpClient
2. Right-click on TimeProviders, and select New > Dword (32-bit) Value.
3. Name it Enabled.
4. Set its value to 0.

Device Metadata Retrieval

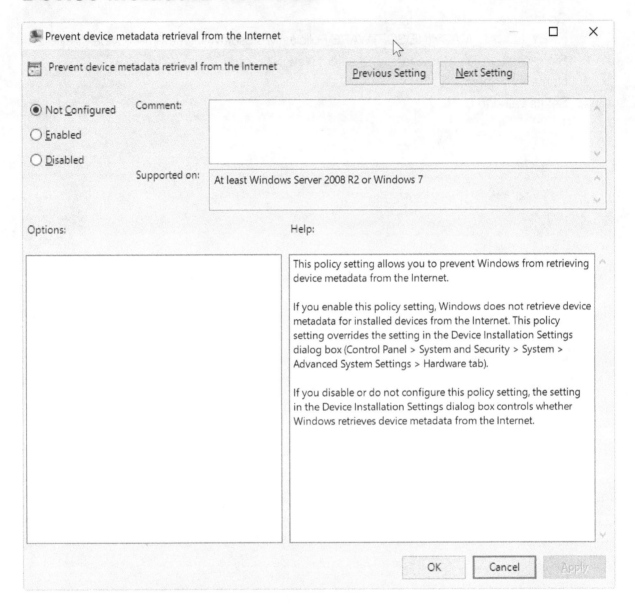

You can prevent Windows from retrieving Device Metadata from the Internet.

If you enable this policy setting, Windows does not retrieve device metadata for installed devices from the Internet. This policy setting overrides the setting in the Device Installation Settings dialog box (Control Panel > System and Security > System > Advanced System Settings > Hardware tab).

This can be configured through policies:

1. Open the Group Policy Editor
2. Go to Computer Configuration > Administrative Templates > System > Device Installation
3. Double-click on "Prevent device metadata retrieval from the Internet.
4. Set the policy to enabled.

Or in the Windows Registry:

1. Open the Windows Registry Editor
2. Go to HKEY_LOCAL_MACHINE\SOFTWARE\Policies\Microsoft\Windows\Device Metadata
3. Right-click on Device Metadata, and select New > Dword (32-bit) Value.
4. Name it PreventDeviceMetadataFromNetwork
5. Set its value to 1.

Font Streaming

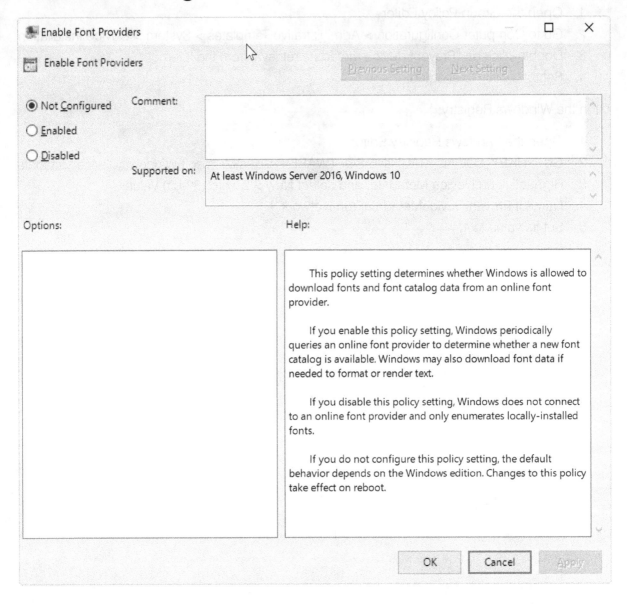

Windows may download fonts on demand that are not stored on the local device. You can disable font streaming in the Registry or through policies

1. Open the Windows Registry Editor
2. Go to HKEY_LOCAL_MACHINE\SOFTWARE\Policies\Microsoft\Windows\System\
3. Right-click on System, and select New > Dword (32-bit) Value.
4. Name it EnableFontProviders
5. Set its value to 1.

Or, by using the Group Policy:

> If you disable this policy setting, Windows does not connect to an online font provider and only enumerates locally-installed fonts.

1. Open the Group Policy Editor.
2. Go to Computer Configuration > Administrative Templates > Network > Fonts
3. Double-click on Enable Font Providers.
4. Set the policy to disabled.

Or, by applying the System\AllowFontProviders MDM policy from the Policy CSP and setting the policy to false to disable font streaming.

Insider Preview Builds

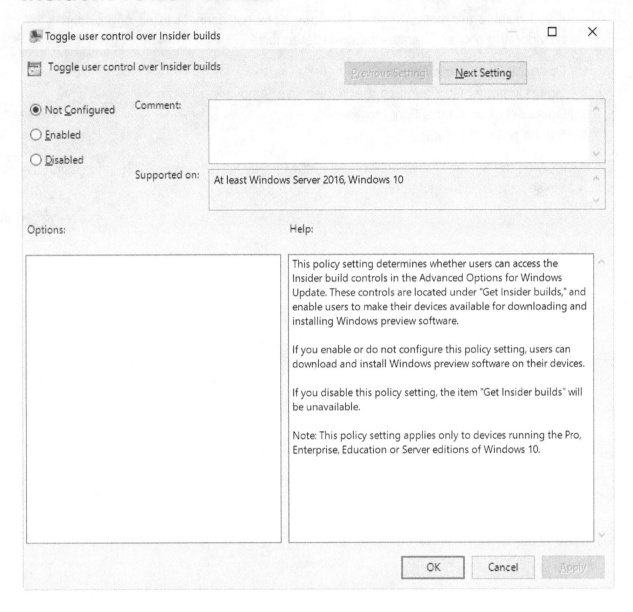

Windows Insider Preview Builds are opt-in test versions of upcoming versions of Windows 10. The setting below prevents checks for new Insider Builds.

It is easy to sign up a machine for joining the Insider program, but not so easy to leave it again.

Note: You need to roll back to a release version of Windows 10 before the following settings can be used.

To turn off Insider Preview Builds for Windows 10:

1. Open the Settings application.

2. Go to Update & security > Windows Insider Program
3. Select Stop Insider Preview builds.

You can turn this off using the Group Policy as well.

> This policy setting determines whether users can access the Insider build controls in the Advanced Options for Windows Update. These controls are located under "Get Insider builds," and enable users to make their devices available for downloading and installing Windows preview software.
>
> If you disable this policy setting, the item "Get Insider builds" will be unavailable.

1. Open the Group Policy Editor.
2. Go to Computer Configuration > Administrative Templates > Windows Components > Data Collection and Preview Builds
3. Select Toggle user control over Insider Builds.
4. Set the policy to Disabled.

You can turn Insider Builds off in the Windows Registry as well:

1. Open the Windows Registry Editor
2. Go to HKEY_LOCAL_MACHINE\SOFTWARE\Policies\Microsoft\Windows\PreviewBuilds
3. Right-click on PreviewBuilds, and select New > Dword (32-bit) Values.
4. Name it AllowBuildPreview
5. Set its value to 0.

You may also apply the System/AllowBuildPreview MDM policy from the Policy CSP. Set it to 0 to prevent users from making their device available for installing preview software.

Microsoft Internet Explorer

Administrators may use the Group Policy to configure various privacy or telemetry related settings.

1. Open the Group Policy.
2. Go to Computer Configuration > Administrative Templates > Windows Components > Internet Explorer.

    1. **Turn on Suggested Sites** – Define whether users may configure suggested sites. Set to disable to turn off.
    2. **Allow Microsoft services to provide enhanced suggestions as user types in the Address Bar** – Select whether users see suggestions when they type in the address bar. Set to disabled to turn off.
    3. **Turn off the auto-complete feature for web addresses** – Choose whether Internet Explorer's auto-complete feature displays matches when users type URLs in the address bar. Set this to enabled to turn it off.
    4. **Turn off browser geolocation** – Choose whether websites may request location data from Internet Explorer. Set to Enabled to turn it off.
    5. **Prevent managing SmartScreen filter** –Select whether users may manage the SmartScreen Filter in Internet Explorer. Default is turned off.

3. Go to User Configuration > Administrative Templates > Windows Components > Internet Explorer > Security Features > Add-on Management

    1. Select **Turn off Automatic download of the ActiveX VersionList** – This policy defines whether Internet Explorer will download updated versions of the VersionList.XML from Microsoft.
    2. Set this policy to enabled.

Warning: Turning off this automatic download breaks the out-of-date ActiveX control blocking feature by not letting the version list update with newly outdated controls, potentially compromising the security of your computer.

It is alternatively possible to configure the settings in the Windows Registry.

1. Open the Windows Registry Editor.
2. For Turn on Suggested Sites:

    1. Go to HKEY_LOCAL_MACHINE\SOFTWARE\Policies\Microsoft\Internet Explorer\ Suggested Sites
    2. Right-click on SuggestedSites, select New > Dword (32-bit) Value.
    3. Set the value to 0.

3. For Allow Microsoft services to provide enhanced suggestions as the user types in the Address Bar

    1. Go to HKEY_LOCAL_MACHINE\SOFTWARE\Policies\Microsoft\Internet Explorer
    2. Right-click on Internet Explorer, and select New > Dword (32-bit) Value.
    3. Name it AllowServicePoweredQSA
    4. Set its value to 0.

4. For Turn off the auto-complete feature for web addresses

    1. Go to HKEY_LOCAL_MACHINE\SOFTWARE\Policies\Microsoft\Explorer\AutoComplete
    2. Right-click on AutoComplete, and select New > String Value.
    3. Name it AutoSuggest
    4. Give it the value No

5. For Turn off browser geolocation

    1. Go to HKEY_LOCAL_MACHINE\SOFTWARE\Policies\Microsoft\Internet Explorer\Geolocation
    2. Right-click on Geolocation, and select New > Dword (32-bit) Value.
    3. Name it PolicyDisableGeolocation
    4. Give it the value 0.

6. For Prevent Managing SmartSCreen Filter

    1. HKEY_LOCAL_MACHINE\SOFTWARE\Policies\Microsoft\ Internet Explorer\PhishingFilter
    2. Right-click on PhishingFilter, and select New > Dword (32-bit) Value.
    3. Name it EnabledV9.
    4. Set its value to 0.

7. For disabling the download of updated ActiveX control lists

    1. HKEY_CURRENT_USER\Software\Microsoft\Internet Explorer\VersionManager
    2. Select DownloadVersionList
    3. Set its value to 0.

Live Tiles

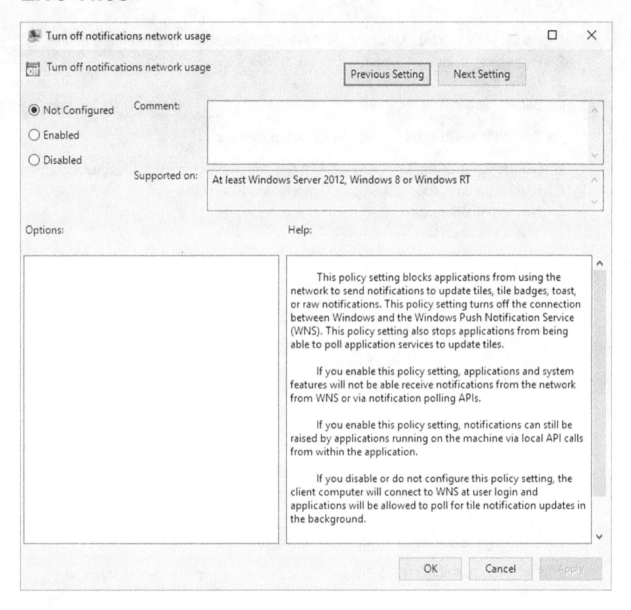

Live Tiles are used by applications. A weather application may display weather information for instance, and pull data from a server on the Internet to update the information.

Turn off network usage of live tiles using the Group Policy

1. Open the Group Policy Editor.
2. Go to User Configuration > Administrative Templates > Start Menu and Taskbar > Notifications
3. Select Turn off notifications network usage.
4. Set the policy to enabled.

This policy setting blocks applications from using the network to send notifications to update tiles, tile badges, toast, or raw notifications. This policy setting turns off the connection between Windows and the Windows Push Notification Service (WNS). This policy setting also stops applications from being able to poll application services to update tiles.

If you enable this policy setting, applications and system features will not be able receive notifications from the network from WNS or via notification polling APIs.

To turn off network usage of Live Tiles using the Windows Registry

Open the Windows Registry Editor.

1. Go to HKEY_CURRENT_USER\SOFTWARE\Policies\Microsoft\Windows\CurrentVersion\ PushNotifications
2. Right-click on PushNotifications, and select New > Dword (32-bit) Value.
3. Name it NoCloudApplicationNotification
4. Set its value to 1

Mail Synchronization

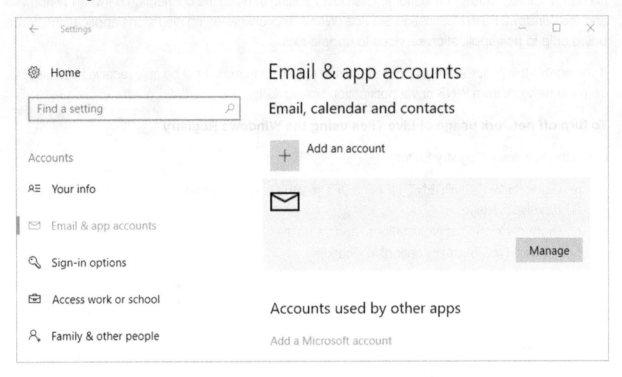

You can turn off mail synchronization for Microsoft Accounts configured on the device.

To turn off Mail Synchronization in the Settings application:

1. Open the Settings application.
2. Go to Accounts > Your email and accounts.
3. Remove any Microsoft Account connected there.

To turn of Mail Synchronization using MDM policy

1. Apply the Accounts/AllowMicrosoftAccountConnection MDM policy from the Policy CSP and set it to 0 to disallow it.

Microsoft Account

Windows 10 users may sign in to the operating system using a Microsoft Account, or a local account. Administrators may block Microsoft Account communication with the Microsoft Account cloud authentication service.

Warning: If you disable this, some apps may lose functionality.

To turn off Microsoft Accounts using the Group Policy

> This policy setting prevents users from adding new Microsoft accounts on this computer.
>
> If you select the "Users can't add Microsoft accounts" option, users will not be able to create new Microsoft accounts on this computer, switch a local account to a Microsoft account, or connect a domain account to a Microsoft account.
>
> If you select the "Users can't add or log on with Microsoft accounts" option, existing Microsoft account users will not be able to log on to Windows. Selecting this option might make it impossible for an existing administrator on this computer to log on and manage the system.

1. Open the Group Policy Editor.
2. Go to Computer Configuration > Windows Settings > Security Settings > Local Policies > Security Options
3. Select Accounts: Block Microsoft Accounts
4. Set it to Users can't add Microsoft accounts

To prevent users from adding Microsoft Accounts using the Registry

1. Open the Windows Registry Editor.
2. Go to HKEY_LOCAL_MACHINE\SOFTWARE\Microsoft\Windows\CurrentVersion\Policies\System
3. Right-click on System, and select New > Dword (32-bit) Value.
4. Name it NoConnectedUser
5. Set its value to 3.

Microsoft Edge

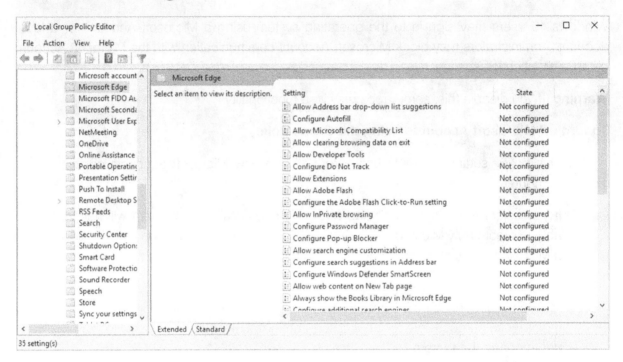

You can control the following features using the Group Policy Editor

1. Open the Group Policy Editor
2. Go to Computer Configuration > Administrative Templates > Windows Components > Microsoft Edge

   1. Configure Autofill – Defines whether users may use autofill functionality.
   2. Configure Do Not Track – Defines whether Do Not Track headers are sent with requests.
   3. Configure Password Manager – Defines whether users may save passwords in Edge.
   4. Configure Search suggestions in Address bar – Defines if suggestions are displayed when users type in the address bar.
   5. Configure Windows Defender SmartScreen Filter – This setting defines whether SmartScreen Filter is turned on or off.
   6. Allow web content on Net Tab Page – Choose whether to display content from the Internet on the browser's New Tab page.
   7. Configure start pages – Set the start page for domain-joined devices.
   8. Prevent First Run webpage from opening in Microsoft Edge – Choose whether a first run page is displayed on first start of Microsoft Edge.

You may configure these features in the Registry as well

1. Open the Windows Registry Editor

    1. Configure Autofill

        1. Go to HKEY_LOCAL_MACHINE\SOFTWARE\Policies\Microsoft\MicrosoftEdge\Main
        2. Right-click on Main, select New > String Value.
        3. Name it Use FormSuggest
        4. Set its value to no.

    2. Configure Do Not Track

        1. Go to HKEY_LOCAL_MACHINE\SOFTWARE\Policies\Microsoft\MicrosoftEdge\Main
        2. Right-click on Main, and select New > Dword (32-bit) Value.
        3. Name it DoNotTrack
        4. Set its value to 1.

    3. Configure Password Manager

        1. Go to HKEY_LOCAL_MACHINE\SOFTWARE\Policies\Microsoft\MicrosoftEdge\Main
        2. Right-click on Main, and select New > String value.
        3. Name it FormSuggest Passwords
        4. Set its value to no.

    4. Configure Search suggestions in Address bar

        1. Go to HKEY_LOCAL_MACHINE\SOFTWARE\Policies\Microsoft\MicrosoftEdge\SearchScopes
        2. Right-click on SearchScopes, and select New > Dword (32-bit) Value.
        3. Name it ShowSearchSuggestionsGlobal
        4. Set its value to 0

    5. Configure Windows Defender SmartScreen Filter

        1. Go to HKEY_LOCAL_MACHINE\SOFTWARE\Policies\Microsoft\MicrosoftEdge\PhishingFilter
        2. Right-click on PhishingFilter, and select New > Dword (32-bit) Value.
        3. Name it EnabledV9
        4. Set its value to 0

6. Allow web content on Net Tab Page – Choose whether to display content from the Internet on the browser's New Tab page.

7. Configure start pages – Set the start page for domain-joined devices.

8. Prevent First Run webpage from opening in Microsoft Edge – Choose whether a first run page is displayed on first start of Microsoft Edge.

Microsoft Edge MDM policies

- Browser/AllowAutoFill
- Browser/AllowDoNotTrack
- Browser/AllowMicrosoftCompatbilityList
- Browser/AllowPasswordManager
- Browser/AllowSearchSuggestionsinAddressBar
- Browser/AllowSmartScreen
- Browser/FirstRunURL

Network Connection Status Indicator

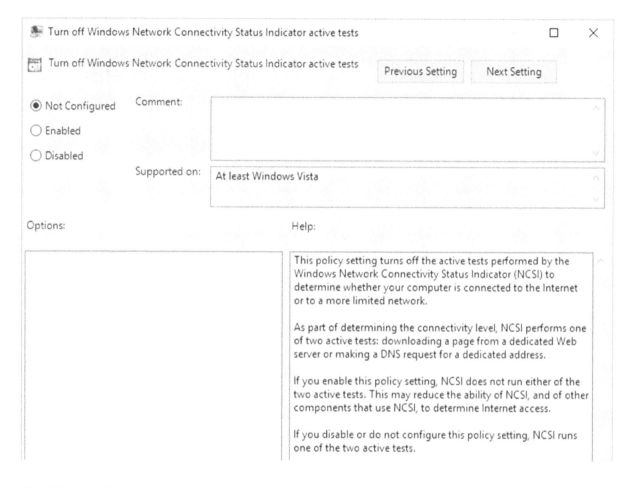

The Network Connection Status Indicator is an automatic test that Windows runs to test Internet connectivity and network connectivity.

It sends a DNS request or a HTTP request to http://www.msftconnecttest.com/connecttest.txt to find out if the device is connected to the Internet.

NCSI can be turned off using the Group Policy

> If you enable this policy setting, NCSI does not run either of the two active tests. This may reduce the ability of NCSI, and of other components that use NCSI, to determine Internet access.

1. Open the Group Policy Editor
2. Go to Computer Configuration > Administrative Templates > System > Internet Communication Management > Internet Communication Settings
3. Open Turn off Windows Network Connectivity Status Indicator active tests.
4. Set the policy to enabled to disable the testing.

You can turn of NCSI using the Windows Registry as well

1. Open the Windows Registry Editor.
2. Go to HKEY_LOCAL_MACHINE\SOFTWARE\Policies\Microsoft\Windows\NetworkConnectivityStatusIndicator
3. Right-click on NetworkConnectivityStatusIndicator, and select New > Dword (32-bit) value.
4. Name it NoActiveProbe.
5. Set its value to 1.

Offline Maps

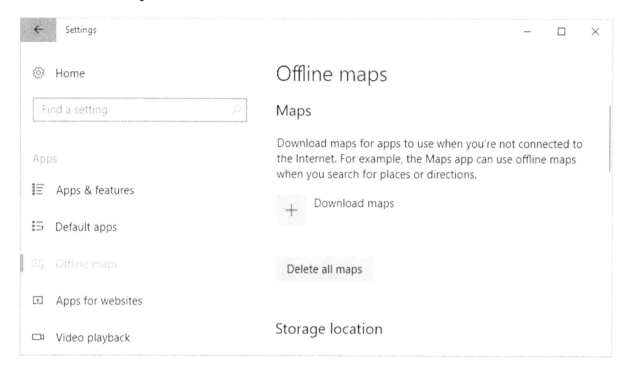

Offline Maps is a feature of the Maps application. You may use it to save maps to the local system, and to update these maps for offline use.

The default Maps application of Windows 10 works similar to Google Maps in many regards. You can use it to browse to locations, find directions, or locate specific buildings on the map.

It supports features such as turn by turn directions, voice guide navigation and more. You may save maps so that they become available even when the device is offline. Useful for situations when Internet connectivity is flaky or not available at all.

Settings application

You can manage offline maps using the Settings application. Go to Settings > Apps > Offline Maps to get started.

You find options on the page to download new maps, to delete existing maps, and configuration options. One of these options lets you define whether maps are updated automatically by Windows.

Toggle "Automatically update maps" on the page to disable the functionality. Note that you only need to configure this if you have downloaded maps actively.

Group Policy

If you enable this setting the automatic download and update of map data is turned off.

1. Open the Group Policy Editor.
2. Go to Computer Configuration > Administrative Templates > Windows Components > Maps
3. Open Turn off Automatic Download and Update of Map Data
4. Set the policy to enabled, to disable the feature on the system.

Windows Registry

Offline Maps can be turned off in the Windows Registry as well.

1. Open the Windows Registry Editor.
2. Go to HKEY_LOCAL_MACHINE\SOFTWARE\Policies\Microsoft\Windows\Maps
3. Right-click on Maps, and select New > Dword (32-bit) Value.
4. Name it AutoDownloadAndUpdateMapData.
5. Give it a value of 0.

OneDrive

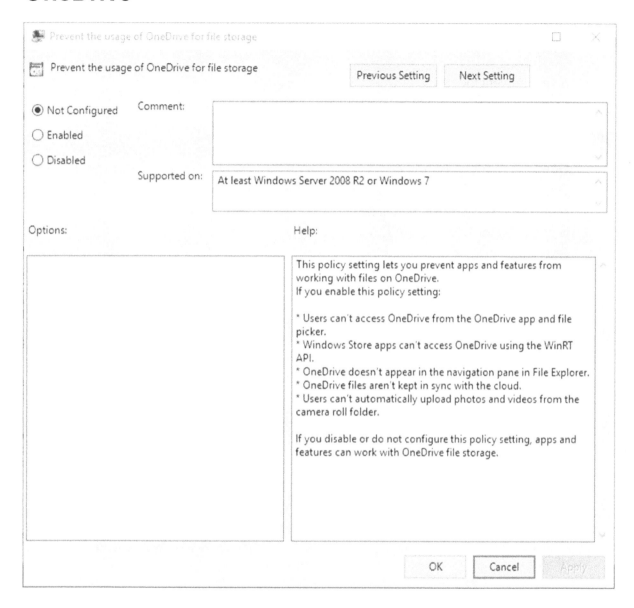

OneDrive, formerly known as SkyDrive, is Microsoft's cloud storage service. OneDrive is integrated in Windows 10 by default.

Disabling OneDrive impacts some functionality, including:

- The camera roll that uploads photos and videos automatically won't work anymore.
- OneDrive files are not kept in sync with cloud servers.
- OneDrive's listing in File Explorer is removed.
- Windows Store applications cannot access OneDrive using the WinRT API.
- Users cannot access OneDrive using the app.

You can turn off OneDrive using the Group Policy

1. Open the Group Policy Editor.
2. Go to Computer Configuration > Administrative Templates > Windows Components > OneDrive
3. Select Prevent the usage of OneDrive for file storage.
4. Set the policy to Enabled.

OneDrive can be turned off using the Windows Registry as well

1. Open the Windows Registry Editor
2. Go to HKEY_LOCAL_MACHINE\SOFTWARE\Policies\Microsoft\Windows\OneDrive
3. Right-click on OneDrive, and select New > Dword (32-bit) Value.
4. Name it DisableFileSyncNGSC
5. Give it the value of 1.

Preinstalled Applications

Windows 10 ships with preinstalled applications. Some of these applications get content before they are opened by users (for a better user experience)

Some of these can be removed using the Settings application, all of them using PowerShell.

Settings application

1. Open the Settings application on the Windows 10 machine.
2. Go to Apps.
3. Click on the application that you want to remove under "Apps & Features".
4. Select uninstall, and follow the instructions.

PowerShell (removing apps for current user)

1. Open an elevated PowerShell command prompt.

2. To remove the Weather app, run: Get-AppxPackage Microsoft.BingWeather | Remove-AppxPackage

3. To remove the Money app, run Get-AppxPackage Microsoft.BingFinance | Remove-AppxPackage

4. To remove the Sports app, run: Get-AppxPackage Microsoft.BingSports | Remove-AppxPackage

5. To remove the Twitter app, run: Get-AppxPackage *.Twitter | Remove-AppxPackage

6. To remove the Xbox app, run: Get-AppxPackage Microsoft.XboxApp | Remove-AppxPackage

7. To remove the Sway app, run: Get-AppxPackage Microsoft.Office.Sway | Remove-AppxPackage

8. To remove the OneNote app, run: Get-AppxPackage Microsoft.Office.OneNote | Remove-AppxPackage

9. To remove the Get Office app, run: Get-AppxPackage Microsoft.MicrosoftOfficeHub | Remove-AppxPackage

10. To remove the Get Skype app, run: Get-AppxPackage Microsoft.SkypeApp | Remove-AppxPackage

11. To remove the Sticky Notes app, run: Get-AppxPackage Microsoft.MicrosoftStickyNotes | Remove-AppxPackage

PowerShell (remove for new users)

1. Open an elevated PowerShell command prompt.

2. To remove the Weather app, run: Get-AppxProvisionedPackage -Online | Where-Object {$_.PackageName -Like "Microsoft.BingWeather"} | ForEach-Object {Remove-AppxProvisionedPackage -Online -PackageName $_.PackageName}

3. To remove the Money app, run Get-AppxProvisionedPackage -Online | Where-Object {$_.PackageName -Like "Microsoft.BingFinance"} | ForEach-Object {Remove-AppxProvisionedPackage -Online -PackageName $_.PackageName}

4. To remove the Sports app, run: Get-AppxProvisionedPackage -Online | Where-Object {$_.PackageName -Like "Microsoft.BingSports"} | ForEach-Object {Remove-AppxProvisionedPackage -Online -PackageName $_.PackageName}

5. To remove the Twitter app, run: Get-AppxProvisionedPackage -Online | Where-Object {$_.PackageName -Like "*.Twitter"} | ForEach-Object {Remove-AppxProvisionedPackage -Online -PackageName $_.PackageName}

6. To remove the Xbox app, run: Get-AppxProvisionedPackage -Online | Where-Object {$_.PackageName -Like "Microsoft.XboxApp"} | ForEach-Object {Remove-AppxProvisionedPackage -Online -PackageName $_.PackageName}

7. To remove the Sway app, run: Get-AppxProvisionedPackage -Online | Where-Object {$_.PackageName -Like "Microsoft.Office.Sway"} | ForEach-Object {Remove-AppxProvisionedPackage -Online -PackageName $_.PackageName}

8. To remove the OneNote app, run: Get-AppxProvisionedPackage -Online | Where-Object {$_.PackageName -Like "Microsoft.Office.OneNote"} | ForEach-Object {Remove-AppxProvisionedPackage -Online -PackageName $_.PackageName}

9. To remove the Get Office app, run: Get-AppxProvisionedPackage -Online | Where-Object {$_.PackageName -Like "Microsoft.MicrosoftOfficeHub"} | ForEach-Object {Remove-AppxProvisionedPackage -Online -PackageName $_.PackageName}

10. 9. To remove the Get Skype app, run: Get-AppxProvisionedPackage -Online | Where-Object {$_.PackageName -Like "Microsoft.SkypeApp"} | ForEach-Object {Remove-AppxProvisionedPackage -Online -PackageName $_.PackageName}

11. To remove the Sticky Notes app, run: Get-AppxProvisionedPackage -Online | Where-Object {$_.PackageName -Like "Microsoft.MicrosoftStickyNotes"} | ForEach-Object {Remove-AppxProvisionedPackage -Online -PackageName $_.PackageName}

Windows 10 Privacy Settings

Windows 10 ships with a dedicated privacy group in the Settings application. You can open it in the following way:

1. Use the keyboard shortcut Windows-I to open the Settings application. You may use the Start menu instead as it links to Settings as well.
2. Select Privacy from the list of available groups.

Notes

- These privacy settings apply only to apps, but not to legacy desktop programs. As a rule of thumb: apps are downloaded from Windows Store, desktop programs are not. This does not apply 100% but to the majority of cases.
- The bulk of settings enable you to allow or disallow access to certain data sets, calendar, contacts, or hardware devices, like the microphone or camera.

The Privacy group of settings lists the following pages in the Windows 10 Creators Update:

- **General** – Lists important privacy settings, and links to look up information and manage information that is stored online.
- **Location** – Manage location based settings such as enabling location-based look-ups, or clearing the location history.
- **Camera** – Select whether apps may use a camera connected to the device, and manage this on a per-app basis.
- **Microphone** – Select whether apps may use the microphone, and manage apps that are allowed to use the microphone.
- **Notifications** – Select whether applications may access notifications, and manage the permission for individual apps.
- **Speech, inking, & typing** – Enable or disable speech services and typing suggestions, and manage cloud information.
- **Account info** – Select whether apps may access your name, picture and other account information, and manage this on a per-application basis.
- **Contacts** – Select whether apps may access your contacts, and manage individual application rights for that.
- **Call history** – Select whether apps may access your call history, and manage these apps individually.
- **Email** – Select whether apps may access your email (including sending), and manage individual application rights.
- **Tasks** – Select whether apps may access tasks, and manage these apps.
- Messaging – Select whether apps may read and send messages (text or MMS), and manage these applications individually.

- **Radios** – Manage radio support, e.g. for Bluetooth and select whether apps are allowed to control radios on the system.
- **Other devices** – Configure app syncing with your other device, and manage the list of trusted devices.
- **Feedback & diagnostics** – Set the Telemetry data level (Basic or Full), set feedback frequency, and toggle the tailored experienced option.
- **Background apps** – Select whether apps are allowed to run in the background, and manage individual app permissions in this regard.
- **App diagnostics** – Select whether apps are allowed to access diagnostic information.
- **Automatic file downloads** – Determines whether file sync services such as OneDrive may download online-only files automatically when requested by the user.

General

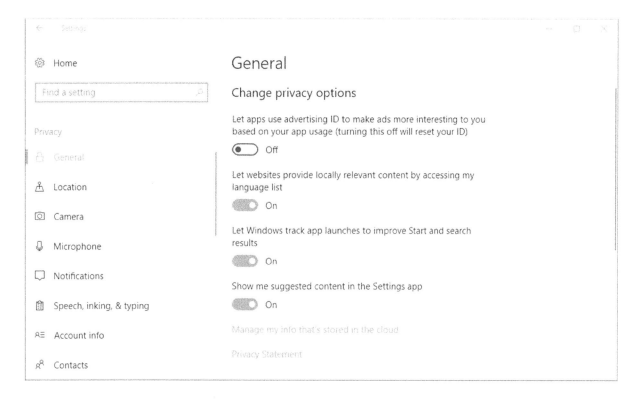

The General page of the Privacy group lists the following options:

- **Let apps use advertising ID to make ads more interesting to you based on your app usage (turning this off will reset your ID)** – This defines whether applications may access the advertising ID that identifies the device which in turn means tracking.

    ◦ Windows generates a unique advertising ID for each user on a device, which app developers and advertising networks can use to provide more relevant advertising in apps. When the advertising ID is enabled, apps can access and use it in much the same way that websites can access and use a unique identifier stored in a cookie. Thus, app developers (and the advertising networks they work with) can use your advertising ID to provide more relevant advertising and other personalized experiences across their apps.

- **Let websites provide locally relevant content by accessing my language list** – Defines whether websites that you open on the device may access the list of languages installed on the device to display local content instead of generic content.

    ◦ Some websites may have their content available in different languages. Windows can share information about your preferred language list with websites so that they can have the opportunity to respect your language preferences without you having to independently set them for each site.

- **Let Windows track app launches to improve Start and search results** – If enabled, Windows tracks application launches and uses the information for Start's (most used apps) and search results.

  ° Windows can personalize your Start menu based on the apps that you launch. This allows you to quickly have access to your list of Most used apps both in the Start menu and when you search your device.

- **Show me suggested content in the Settings application** – Windows 10 may display suggestions, read tips and promotions, in the Settings application when not turned off.

Advertising ID

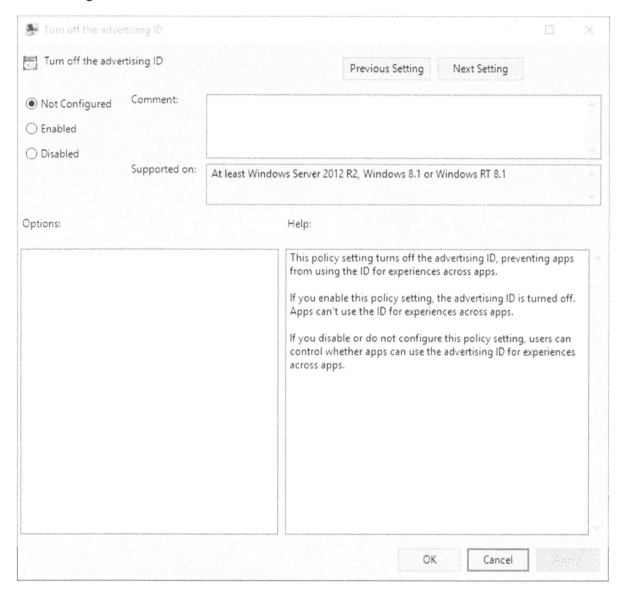

Note: The advertising ID is reset when you turn off the feature in the UI.

Group Policy options

1. Open the Group Policy Editor
2. Go to Computer Configuration > Administrative Templates > System > User Profiles
3. Select Turn off the advertising ID.
4. Set the policy to enabled.

Registry options

1. Open the Windows Registry Editor
2. Go to HKEY_LOCAL_MACHINE\SOFTWARE\Microsoft\Windows\CurrentVersion\AdvertisingInfo
3. Right-click on AdvertisingInfo and select New > Dword (32-bit) Value.
4. Name it Enabled.
5. Set its value to 0.

or,

6. Go to HKEY_LOCAL_MACHINE\SOFTWARE\Policies\Microsoft\Windows\AdvertisingInfo
7. Right-click on AdvertisingInfo, and select New > Dword (32-bit) Value.
8. Name it DisabledByGroupPolicy
9. Set its value to 1.

Let websites provide locally relevant content by accessing my language list

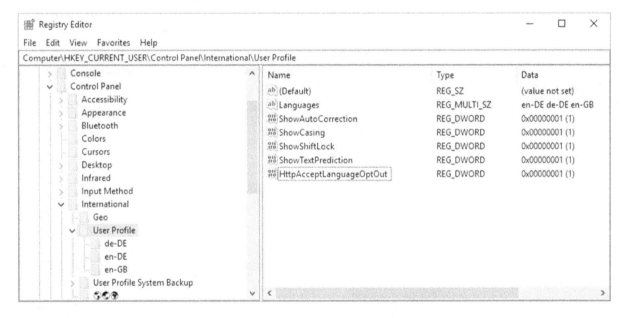

1. Open the Windows Registry Editor.
2. Go to HKEY_CURRENT_USER\Control Panel\International\User Profile
3. Right-click on User Profile, and select New > Dword (32-bit) Value from the context menu.
4. Name it HttpAcceptLanguageOptOut
5. Set its value to 1.

Let Windows track app launches to improve Start and search results

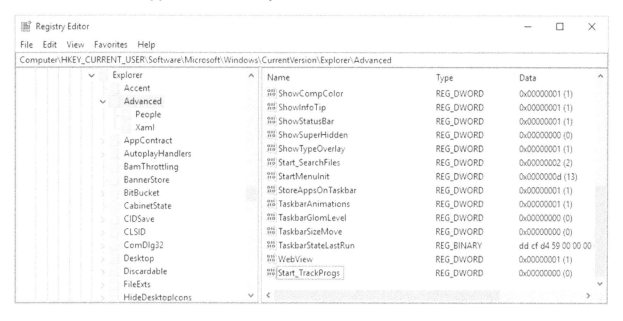

1. Open the Windows Registry Editor.
2. HKEY_CURRENT_USER\SOFTWARE\Microsoft\Windows\CurrentVersion\Explorer\
   Advanced
3. Right-click on Advanced, select New > Dword (32-bit) Value.
4. Name it Start_TrackProgs
5. Set its value to 0.

Location

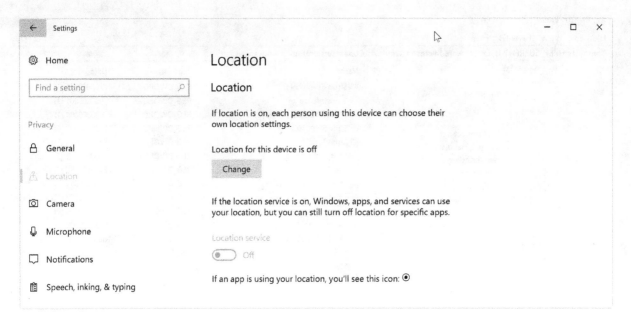

The following options are available when you open the Location group of the Privacy Settings application:

- **Location on / off** – This toggle allows you to enable or disable location functionality on the device. If disabled, no application that runs on the device may make use of it.
- **Default location** – You may add a default location which Windows, apps and services will make use of it no location cannot be detected.
- **Location history** – Windows 10 stores the location history for a limited period of time (24 hours) on the device. You may use this option to clear the location history on the device.
- **Choose apps that can use your precise location** – Select individual applications that are allowed to look up your location.
- **Geofencing** – Lists applications that make use of Geofencing.

  ◦ Some apps use geofencing, which can turn on or off particular services or show you information that might be useful when you're in an area defined (or "fenced") by the app

To turn off Location for this Device

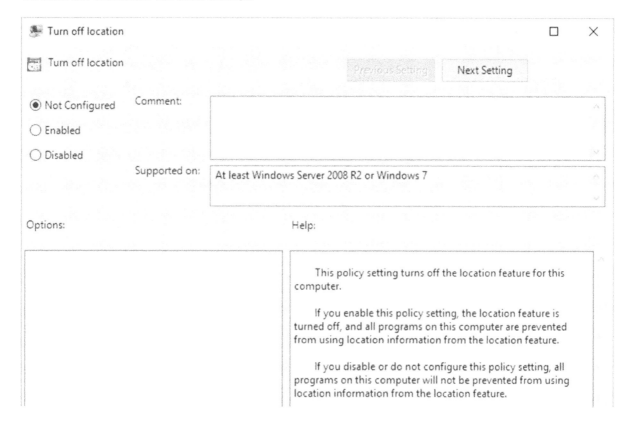

Group Policy

If you enable this policy setting, the location feature is turned off, and all programs on this computer are prevented from using location information from the location feature.

1. Open the Group Policy Editor
2. Go to Computer Configuration > Administrative Templates > Windows Components > Location and Sensors
3. Select Turn off Location.
4. Set the policy to enabled, to disable location on the device.

Windows Registry Editor

1. Open the Registry Editor
2. Go to HKEY_LOCAL_MACHINE\Software\Policies\Microsoft\Windows\AppPrivacy
3. Right-click on AppPrivacy, and select New > Dword (32-bit) Value.

4. Name it LetAppsAccessLocation

    1. Set the value to 1 to turn on application location access, and users cannot change it.

    2. Set its value to 2 to turn off location access, and disallow users to change it.

MDM policy from the Policy CSP (System/AllowLocation)

- 0 means it is turned off, and users can't turn it back on.
- 1 means it is turned on, but users may turn it off.
- 2 means it is turned on, and users can't turn it off.

To turn off Location for apps

Group Policy

This policy setting specifies whether Windows apps can access location.

You can specify either a default setting for all apps or a per-app setting by specifying a Package Family Name. You can get the Package Family Name for an app by using

the Get-AppPackage Windows PowerShell cmdlet. A per-app setting overrides the default setting.

If you choose the "Force Deny" option, Windows apps are not allowed to access location and employees in your organization cannot change it.

1. Open the Group Policy Editor
2. Go to Computer Configuration > Administrative Templates > Windows Components > App Privacy
3. Select Let Windows apps access location.
4. Enable the policy.
5. Set the "default for all apps" box to Force Deny.

Windows Registry

1. Open the Registry Editor
2. Go to HKEY_LOCAL_MACHINE\Software\Policies\Microsoft\Windows\LocationAndSensors
3. Right-click on LocationAndSensors, and select New > Dword (32-bit) Value.
4. Name it DisableLocation
5. Set its value to 1.

Related Preferences

Turn off location

This setting determines whether the location feature is available on this device.

Policy: Computer Configuration > Administrative Templates > Windows Components > Location and Sensors > Turn off location

- Enabled – Location feature is turned off, and all programs on the computer are prevented from using the location feature.
- Disabled – Same as not configured; the location feature is enabled.

Windows Registry

Key: HKEY_LOCAL_MACHINE\Policies\Microsoft\Windows\AppPrivacy

Name: LetAppsAccessLocation

Type: Dword

- 2 – Turned off

Turn off location scripting

This feature turns off scripting for the location feature (means whether scripts for the location feature may run).

Policy: Computer Configuration > Administrative Templates > Windows Components > Location and Sensors > Turn off location scripting

- Enabled – This turns location scripting off so that it is not available.
- Disabled – Same as not configured; location scripting is enabled.

Windows Registry

Key: HKEY_LOCAL_MACHINE\SOFTWARE\Policies\Microsoft\Windows\LocationAndSensors

Name: DisableLocationScripting

Type: Dword

- 0 – The feature is enabled.
- 1 – The feature is disabled.

Camera

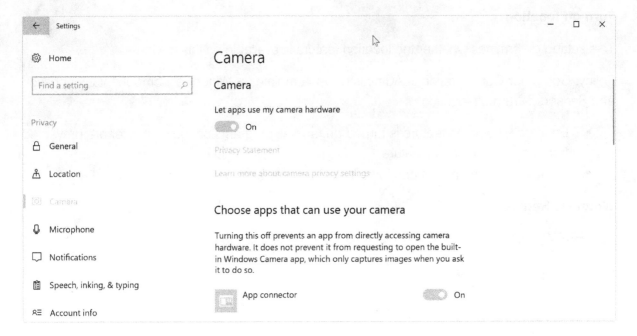

The Camera privacy group offers the following options:

- Toggle the use of camera hardware (e.g. a webcam), by apps on or off.
- Manage all applications that may use the camera, and allow or disallow usage individually.

General information on camera use:

Windows 10 highlights the use of the camera by turning on the camera light whenever it is in use.

If the device does not have a camera light, a notification is displayed instead.

Some exceptions apply to the general camera privacy settings. Windows Hello, Windows 10's biometric authentication system, will make use of the camera even if camera use is disabled for applications in the privacy settings.

The setting ignores desktop programs. Only Windows Store apps and apps that ship with Windows 10 by default are affected by the settings.

Let apps use my camera

Let Windows apps access the camera   □   ✕

Let Windows apps access the camera

                                   Previous Setting   Next Setting

◉ Not Configured   Comment:

○ Enabled

○ Disabled

                 Supported on: At least Windows Server, Windows 10

Options: Help:

Default for all apps:

Put user in control of these specific apps (use Package Family Names):

Force allow these specific apps (use Package Family Names):

Force deny these specific apps (use Package Family Names):

This policy setting specifies whether Windows apps can access the camera.

You can specify either a default setting for all apps or a per-app setting by specifying a Package Family Name. You can get the Package Family Name for an app by using the Get-AppPackage Windows PowerShell cmdlet. A per-app setting overrides the default setting.

If you choose the "User is in control" option, employees in your organization can decide whether Windows apps can access the camera by using Settings > Privacy on the device.

If you choose the "Force Allow" option, Windows apps are allowed to access the camera and employees in your organization cannot change it.

If you choose the "Force Deny" option, Windows apps are not allowed to access the camera and employees in your organization cannot change it.

If you disable or do not configure this policy setting, employees in your organization can decide whether Windows apps can access the camera by using Settings > Privacy on the device.

If an app is open when this Group Policy object is applied on a device, employees must restart the app or device for the policy

                                        OK   Cancel   Apply

Group Policy

This policy setting specifies whether Windows apps can access the camera.

You can specify either a default setting for all apps or a per-app setting by specifying a Package Family Name. You can get the Package Family Name for an app by using

the Get-AppPackage Windows PowerShell cmdlet. A per-app setting overrides the default setting.

1. Open the Group Policy Editor
2. Go to Computer Configuration > Administrative Templates > Windows Components > App Privacy
3. Select Let Windows apps access the camera.
4. Set the policy to enabled.
5. In the "Default for all apps" box, select one of the following values:

   1. User is in control means that users may allow or disallow access to the camera using the Settings application.
   2. Force Allow means that apps may access the camera, and that users cannot change this.
   3. Force Deny means that apps cannot access the camera, and that users cannot change this.

Windows Registry

1. Open the Registry Editor
2. Go to HKEY_LOCAL_MACHINE\Software\Policies\Microsoft\Windows\AppPrivacy
3. Right-click on AppPrivacy, and select New > Dword (32-bit) Value.
4. Name it LetAppsAccessCamera.
5. Set the value to one of the following supported integers:

   1. A value of 0 means that the user is in control.
   2. A value of 1 means force allow.
   3. A value of 2 means force deny.

MDM policy from the Policy CSP (Camera/AllowCamera)

1. Value of 0 means apps cannot use camera.
2. Value of 1 means apps may use the camera.

Microphone

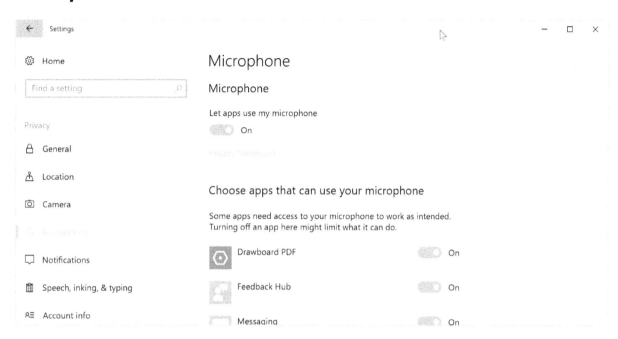

The Microphone privacy settings page offers the following options:

- Toggle microphone use by applications. If turned off, applications may not use the microphone for functionality.
- Select permissions for applications individually.

As is the case with the camera preference, the microphone preference affects only Windows Applications but not desktop programs.

Let apps use my microphone

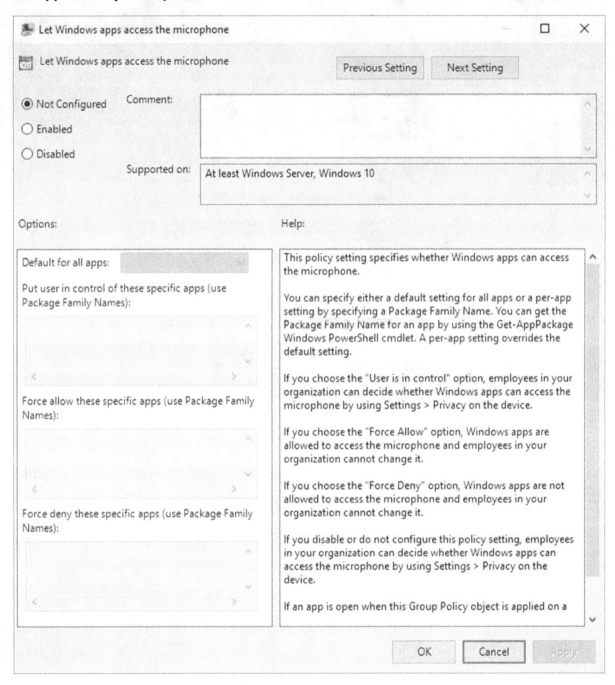

Group Policy

This policy setting specifies whether Windows apps can access the microphone.

You can specify either a default setting for all apps or a per-app setting by specifying a Package Family Name. You can get the Package Family Name for an app by using

the Get-AppPackage Windows PowerShell cmdlet. A per-app setting overrides the default setting.

1. Open the Group Policy Editor
2. Go to Computer Configuration > Administrative Templates > Windows Components > App Privacy
3. Select Let windows apps access the microphone
4. Set the policy to enabled.
5. In the "default for all apps" box, set one of the following values:

   1. User is in control means that users may change the privacy setting using the Settings application.
   2. Force allow means that apps may access the microphone, and that users cannot change it.
   3. Force deny means that apps may not access the microphone, and that users cannot change this.

Windows Registry

1. Open the Registry Editor
2. Go to HKEY_LOCAL_MACHINE\Software\Policies\Microsoft\Windows\AppPrivacy
3. Right-click on AppPrivacy, and select New > Dword (32-bit) Value.
4. Name it LetAppsAccessMicrophone.
5. Set it to one of the following values:

   1. A value of 0 means that users are in control.
   2. A value of 1 means force allow.
   3. A value of 2 means force deny.

MDM policy from the Policy CSP (Privacy/LetAppsAccessMicrophone)

- Value of 0: user is in control.
- Value of 1: force allow
- Value of 2: force deny.

Notifications

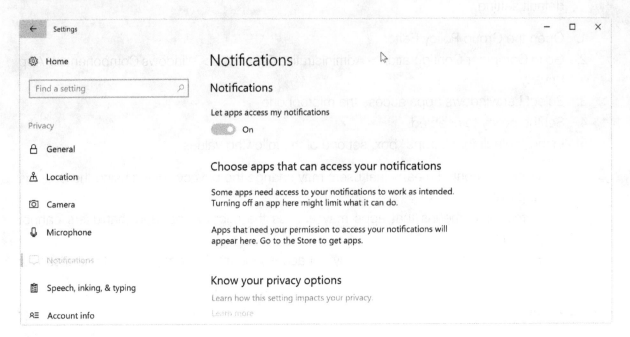

The Notifications page provides you with two options:

- Enable or disable notifications.
- Manage notifications for applications individually.

Let apps access my notifications

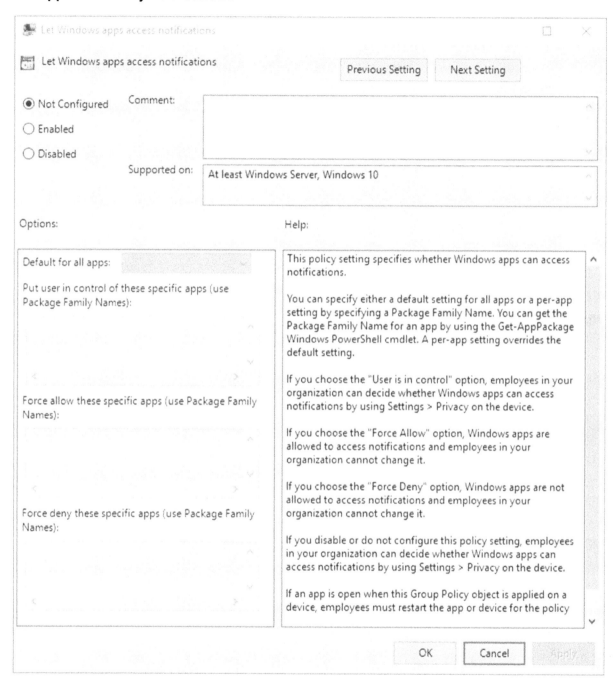

Group Policy

This policy setting specifies whether Windows apps can access notifications.

You can specify either a default setting for all apps or a per-app setting by specifying a Package Family Name. You can get the Package Family Name for an app by using

the Get-AppPackage Windows PowerShell cmdlet. A per-app setting overrides the default setting.

1. Open the Group Policy Editor.
2. Go to Computer Configuration > Administrative Templates > Windows Components > App Privacy.
3. Select Let Windows apps access notifications.
4. Set the policy to enabled.
5. Set the "default for all apps" box to one of the following values:

   1. User is in control means that users can control the access to notifications using the Settings application.
   2. Force allow means that apps are allowed to access notifications, and that users cannot change that.
   3. Force deny means that apps are not allowed to access notifications, and that users cannot change that.

Windows Registry

1. Open the Registry Editor.
2. Go to HKEY_LOCAL_MACHINE\Software\Policies\Microsoft\Windows\AppPrivacy
3. Right-click on AppPrivacy, and select New > Dword (32-bit) Value.
4. Name it LetAppsAccessNotifications.
5. Set it to one of the following values:

   1. A value of 0 means that the user is in control of the functionality.
   2. A value of 1 means force allow.
   3. A value of 2 means force deny.

MDM policy from the Policy CSP (Privacy/LetAppsAccessNotifications)

- Value of 0: user is in control.
- Value of 1: force allow
- Value of 2: force deny.

Speech, inking & typing

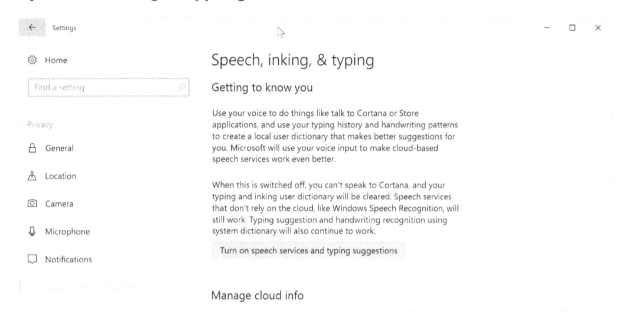

Speech services and typing suggestions can be turned on or off when you open the speech, inking & typing page of the privacy options.

When switched on, it enables you to talk to Cortana and other Store applications. Your typing history and handwriting patterns are used to create a local user dictionary, and provide you with better suggestions

Microsoft will use voice input to improve cloud-based speech services

When the setting is off, you cannot talk to Cortana, and any existing typing and inking user dictionary is erased. Voice data in the cloud is disassociated with the device.

Speech services that don't rely on the cloud will still work, and so will typing suggestions and handwriting recognition that uses the system dictionary.

> *To use speech recognition, getting to know you (the privacy setting under Speech, inking & typing) must be turned on because speech services exist both in the cloud and on your device. The info Microsoft collects from these services helps to improve them. Speech services that don't rely on the cloud and only live on your device, like Narrator and Windows Speech Recognition, will still work when this setting is turned off, but Microsoft won't collect any speech data.*
>
> *When your Diagnostic and usage data setting (Settings > Privacy > Feedback & diagnostics) is set to Full, your inking and typing input*

data is sent to Microsoft, and we use this data in the aggregate to improve the inking and typing platform for all users. Learn more about Diagnostic data here. As part of inking and typing on your device, Windows creates a user dictionary that stores unique words like names you write, which helps you type and ink more accurately.

Turn off automatic learning

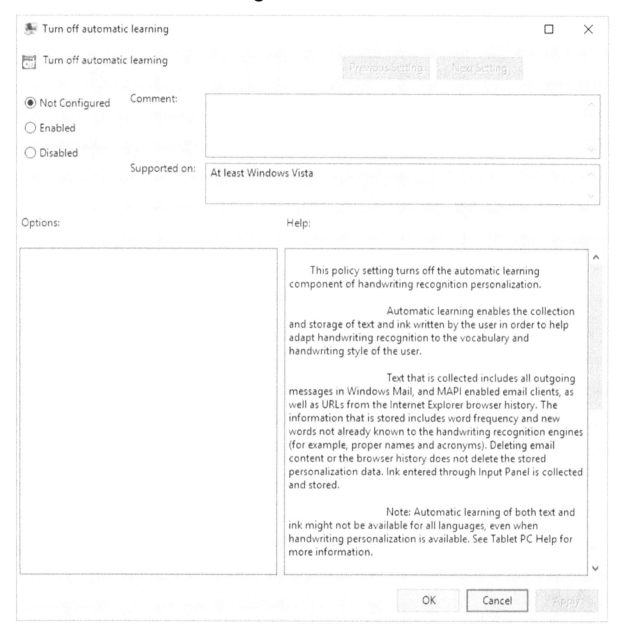

Automatic learning enables the collection and storage of text and ink written by the user in order to help adapt handwriting recognition to the vocabulary and handwriting style of the user.

Text that is collected includes all outgoing messages in Windows Mail, and MAPI enabled email clients, as well as URLs from the Internet Explorer browser history. The information that is stored includes word frequency and new words not already known to the handwriting recognition engines (for example, proper names and acronyms). Deleting email content or the browser history does not delete the stored personalization data. Ink entered through Input Panel is collected and stored.

Group Policy

This policy setting turns off the automatic learning component of handwriting recognition personalization.

If you enable this policy setting, automatic learning stops and any stored data is deleted. Users cannot configure this setting in Control Panel.

1. Open the Group Policy Editor.
2. Go to Computer Configuration > Administrative Templates > Control Panel > Regional and Language Options > Handwriting personalization
3. Select Turn off automatic learning.
4. Set the policy to enabled.

Registry Editor

1. Open the Windows Registry Editor
2. Go to HKEY_LOCAL_MACHINE\Policies\Microsoft\InputPersonalization
3. Right-click on InputPersonalization, and select New > Dword (32-bit) Value.
4. Name it RestrictImplicitInkCollection.
5. Set its value to 1.

or

1. Go to HKEY_CURRENT_USER\SOFTWARE\Microsoft\Personalization\Settings.
2. Right-click on Settings, and select New > Dword (32-bit) Value.
3. Name it AcceptedPrivacyPolicy.
4. Set its value to 0.

or

1. Go to HKEY_CURRENT_USER\SOFTWARE\Microsoft\InputPersonalization\TrainedDataStore
2. Right-click on TrainedDataStore, and select New > Dword (32-bit) Value.
3. Name it HarvestContacts
4. Set its value to 0.

Allow Input Personalization

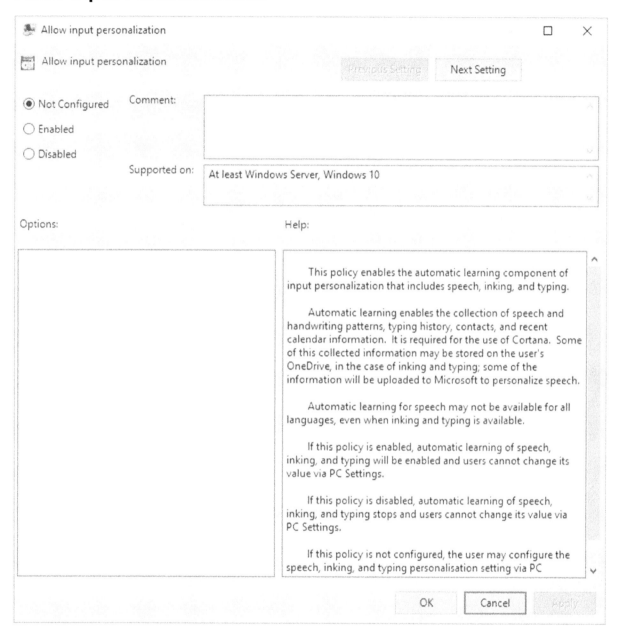

Group Policy

This policy turns of the automatic learning component of input personalization (that includes speech, inking and typing).

> Automatic learning enables the collection of speech and handwriting patterns, typing history, contacts, and recent calendar information. It is required for the use of Cortana. Some of this collected information may be stored on the user's

OneDrive, in the case of inking and typing; some of the information will be uploaded to Microsoft to personalize speech.

Policy: Computer Configuration > Administrative Templates > Control Panel > Regional and Language Options > Allow input personalization

- Enabled – Automatic learning of speech, inking and typing is enabled. Some information may be uploaded to Microsoft, and some may be stored on OneDrive.
- Disabled – The feature is turned off. Automatic learning of speech, typing and inking is stopped.

Windows Registry

Key: HKEY_CURRENT_USER\SOFTWARE\Microsoft\InputPersonalization

Name: RestrictImplicitTextCollection

Type: Dword

- 1 – Turn off implicit text collection.
- 0 – Default, text is collected.

Key: HKEY_CURRENT_USER\SOFTWARE\Microsoft\InputPersonalization

Name: RestrictImplicitInkCollection

Type: Dword

- 1 – Turn off implicit ink collection.
- 0 – Default, ink data is collected.

Key: HKEY_CURRENT_USER\SOFTWARE\Microsoft\InputPersonalization\TrainedDataStore

Name: HarvestContacts

Type: Dword

- 0 – The feature is turned off.
- 1 – Default, the feature is enabled.

Turn off updates to speech recognition and speech synthesis

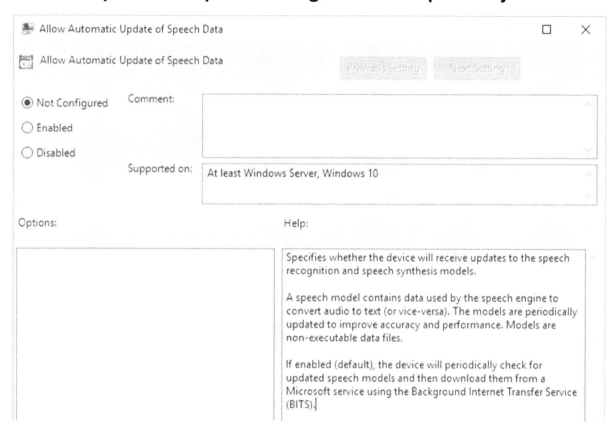

Determines whether the device will check for speech recognition and speech synthesis updates, and download them automatically.

Group Policy

> A speech model contains data used by the speech engine to convert audio to text (or vice-versa). The models are periodically updated to improve accuracy and performance. Models are non-executable data files.
>
> If enabled (default), the device will periodically check for updated speech models and then download them from a Microsoft service using the Background Internet Transfer Service (BITS).

1. Open the Group Policy Editor.
2. Go to Computer Configuration > Administrative Templates > Windows Components > Speech
3. Select Allow automatically update of Speech Data
4. Set the policy to disabled.

Windows Registry

1. Open the Windows Registry Editor
2. Go to HKEY_LOCAL_MACHINE\SOFTWARE\Microsoft\Speech_OneCore\Preferences
3. Right-click on Preferences, and select New > Dword (32-bit) Value.
4. Name it ModelDownloadAllowed.
5. Set the value to 0.

MDM policy from the Policy CSP (Speech/AllowSpeechModelUpdate)

- A value of 0 means not allowed.
- A value of 1 means allowed.

Turn off handwriting personalization data sharing

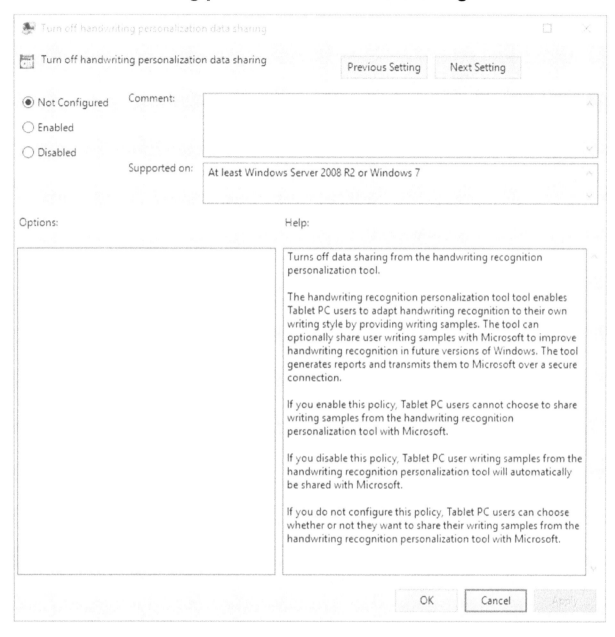

The handwriting recognition personalization tool may be used on Windows Tablet PCs to adapt handwriting recognition to the user's writing style.

Windows Tablet PCs may share handwriting data automatically with Microsoft to "improve handwriting recognition in future versions of Windows".

Group Policy

Computer Configuration > Administrative Templates > System > Internet Communication Management > Internet Communication settings > Turn off handwriting personalization data sharing

- Enabled: When this policy is enabled Windows users may not share writing samples from the handwriting recognition personalization tool with Microsoft.
- Disabled: Samples are shared automatically with Microsoft when the tool is being used.
- Not Configured: Users are prompted and may decide to share the data with Microsoft.

Windows Registry

Registry Key: HKEY_LOCAL_MACHINE \SOFTWARE\Policies\Microsoft\Windows\TabletPC

Name: PreventHandwritingDataSharing

Type: Dword

- A value of 1 prevents handwriting data sharing.

Turn off handwriting recognition error reporting

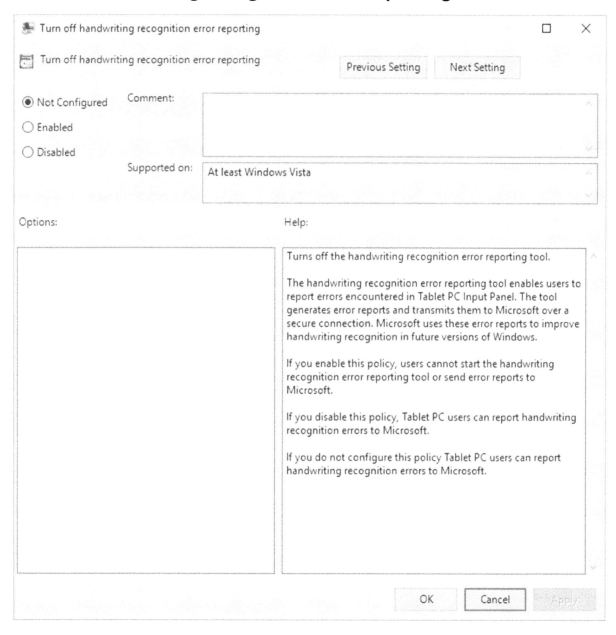

The handwriting recognition error reporting tool enables users to report errors. The tool generates error reports, and transmits them to Microsoft.

Microsoft uses the data to improve handwriting recognition in future versions of Windows.

Group Policy

Computer Configuration > Administrative Templates > System > Internet Communication Management > Internet Communication settings > Turn off handwriting recognition error reporting

- Enabled: When this policy is enabled, users may not start the handwriting recognition error reporting tool or send error reports to Microsoft.
- Disabled: Same as not configured. Users may use the handwriting recognition error reporting tool to send error data to Microsoft.

Windows Registry

Registry Key: HKEY_LOCAL_MACHINE \SOFTWARE\Policies\Microsoft\Windows\Handwriting ErrorReports

Name: PreventHandwritingErrorReports

Type: Dword

- A value of 1 prevents use of the handwriting error reporting tool, and the reporting of errors to Microsoft.

Account Info

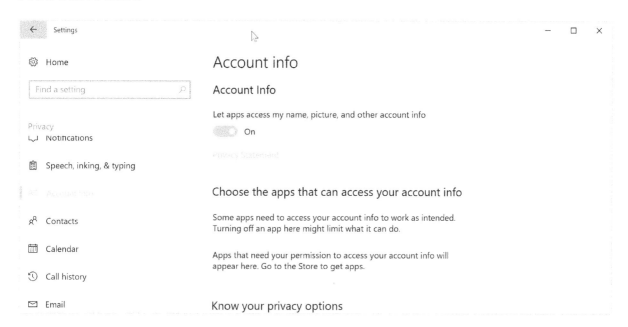

The Account info page provides you with the means to enable or disable general access to your name, picture and other account information.

You may also allow or disallow access on a per-application basis instead.

Let apps access my name, picture, and other account info

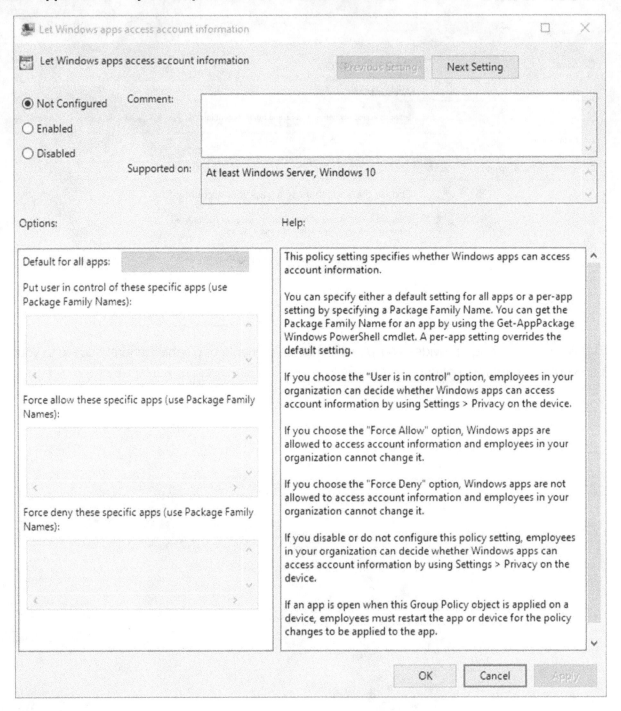

Group Policy

This policy setting specifies whether Windows apps can access account information.

You can specify either a default setting for all apps or a per-app setting by specifying a Package Family Name. You can get the Package Family Name for an app by using the Get-AppPackage Windows PowerShell cmdlet. A per-app setting overrides the default setting.

If you choose the "Force Deny" option, Windows apps are not allowed to access account information and employees in your organization cannot change it.

1. Load the Group Policy Editor.
2. Go to Computer Configuration > Administrative Templates > Windows Components > App Privacy.
3. Open Let Windows apps access account information.
4. Set the policy to enabled.
5. Set the "default for all apps" setting to one of the following values:

    1. User is in control means that users may select to allow or block individual apps, or the privacy feature, in the Settings application.
    2. Force Allow means that Windows apps may use account information, and that users cannot change that.
    3. Force Deny means that Windows apps may not use account information, and that users cannot change that.

Windows Registry

1. Open the Windows Registry Editor.
2. Go to HKEY_LOCAL_MACHINE\SOFTWARE\Policies\Microsoft\Windows\AppPrivacy.
3. Right-click on AppPrivacy, and select New > Dword (32-bit) Value from the menu.
4. Name the new value LetAppsAccessAccountInfo
5. Set its value to one of the following supported values:

    1. Value of 0 means user is in control.
    2. Value of 1 means force allow.
    3. Value of 2 means force deny.

MDM policy from the Policy CSP (Privacy/LetAppsAccessAccountInfo)

- A value of 0 means the user is in control.
- A value of 1 means force allow.
- A value of 2 means force deny.

Contacts

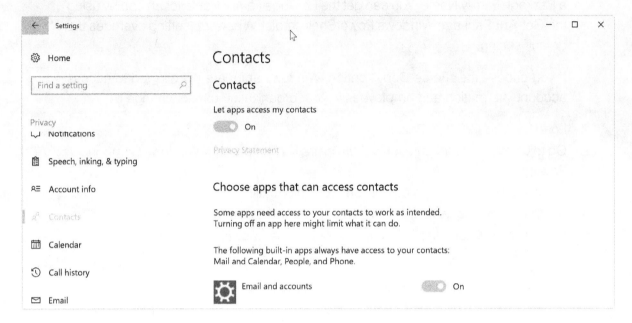

The Contacts privacy page lists two main options right now:

- Enable or disable access to contacts by applications.
- Manage access rights to contacts for individual applications.

Choose apps that can access contacts

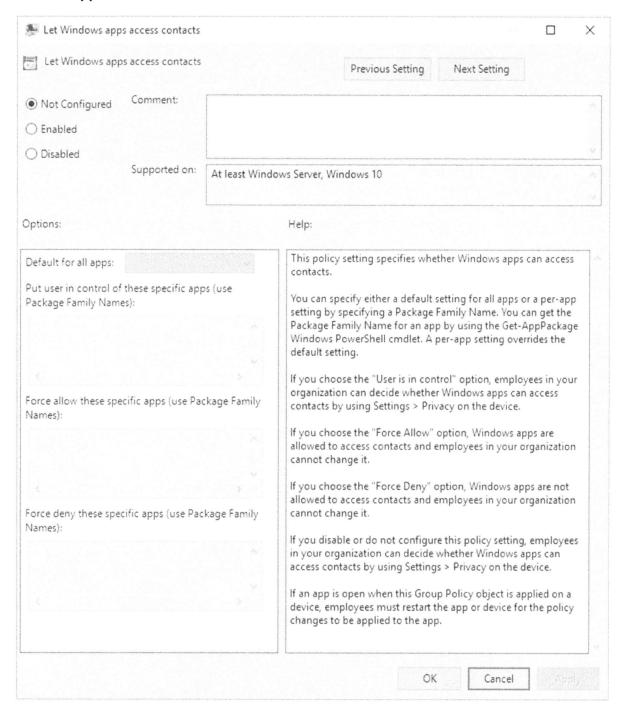

Group Policy

This policy setting specifies whether Windows apps can access contacts.

You can specify either a default setting for all apps or a per-app setting by specifying a Package Family Name. You can get the Package Family Name for an app by using the Get-AppPackage Windows PowerShell cmdlet. A per-app setting overrides the default setting.

1. Open the Group Policy Editor.
2. Go to Computer Configuration > Administrative Templates > Windows Components > App Privacy.
3. Open the Let Windows apps access contacts policy.
4. Enable the policy.
5. Set the "default for all apps" setting to one of the following values

    1. User is in control gives users options to allow or disallow apps to access contacts.
    2. Force allow means that applications may access contacts, and that users cannot prevent this.
    3. Force deny means that applications may not access contacts, and that users cannot allow them.

Windows Registry

1. Open the Windows Registry Editor
2. Go to HKEY_LOCAL_MACHINE\SOFTWARE\Policies\Microsoft\Windows\AppPrivacy
3. If the Dword value LetAppsAccessContacts does not exist, right-click on AppPrivacy, and select New > Dword (32-bit) Value from the context menu, and name it accordingly.
4. Set the preference to 2 to disable access to contacts.

MDM policy from the Policy CSP (Privacy/LetAppsAccessContacts)

- A value of 0 means the user is in control.
- A value of 1 means force allow.
- A value of 2 means force deny.

Calendar

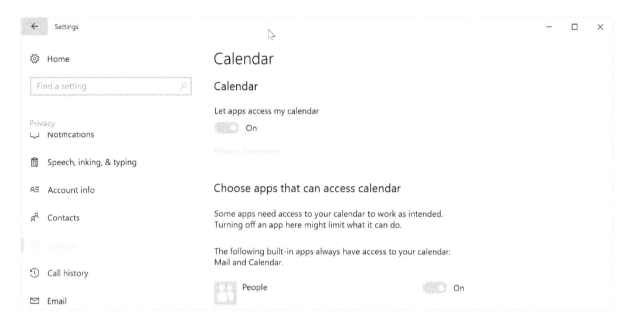

You may use the Calendar page of the privacy settings to allow or disallow application access to the calendar.

You may furthermore allow or disallow access to the calendar for individual applications.

Let apps access the calendar

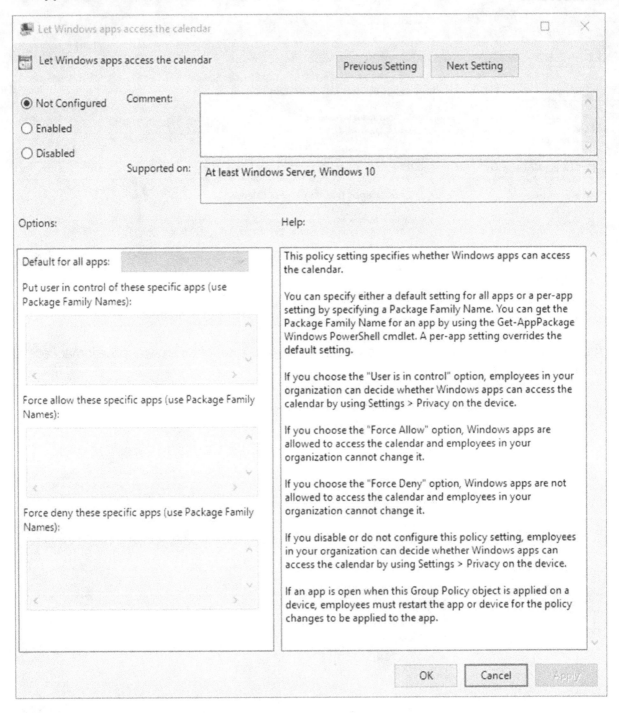

Group Policy

This policy setting specifies whether Windows apps can access the calendar.

You can specify either a default setting for all apps or a per-app setting by specifying a Package Family Name. You can get the Package Family Name for an app by using the Get-AppPackage Windows PowerShell cmdlet. A per-app setting overrides the default setting.

1. Load the Group Policy Editor.
2. Go to Computer Configuration > Administrative Templates > Windows Components > App Privacy.
3. Open Let Windows apps access the calendar
4. Set the policy to enabled.
5. Set the "default for all apps" setting to one of the following values:

   1. User is in control means that users may allow or block apps to access the calendar.
   2. Force allow means that apps may access calendar data, and that users cannot block this.
   3. Force deny means that apps may not access calendar data, and that users cannot block this.

Windows Registry

1. Open the Windows Registry Editor.
2. Go to HKEY_LOCAL_MACHINE\SOFTWARE\Policies\Microsoft\Windows\AppPrivacy.
3. Right-click on AppPrivacy, and select New > Dword (32-bit) Value from the menu.
4. Name the new value **LetAppsAccessCalendar.**
5. Set its value to one of the following values:

   1. Value of 0 means user is in control.
   2. Value of 1 means force allow.
   3. Value of 2 means force deny.

MDM policy from the Policy CSP (Privacy/LetAppsAccessCalendar)

- A value of 0 means the user is in control.
- A value of 1 means force allow.
- A value of 2 means force deny.

Call History

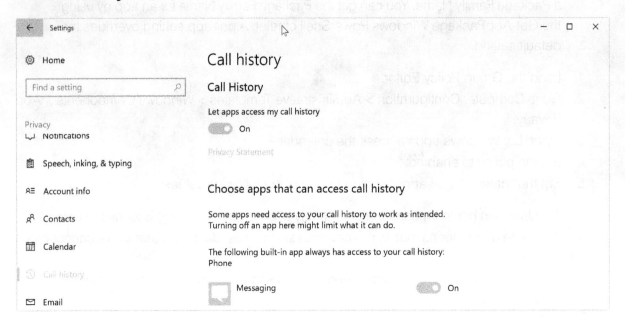

The Call History, just like most of the other privacy settings, provides you with two options:

- Allow or disallow access to the Call History for all applications.
- Allow or disallow individual application access to the Call History.

Let apps access my call history

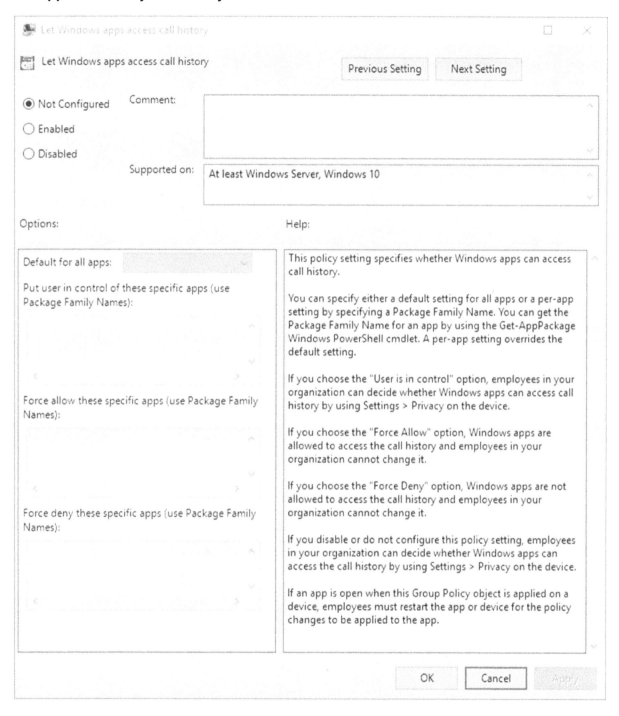

Group Policy

This policy setting specifies whether Windows apps can access call history.

You can specify either a default setting for all apps or a per-app setting by specifying a Package Family Name. You can get the Package Family Name for an app by using the Get-AppPackage Windows PowerShell cmdlet. A per-app setting overrides the default setting.

1. Open the Group Policy Editor.
2. Go to Computer Configuration > Administrative Templates > Windows Components > App Privacy
3. Open Let Windows apps access call history.
4. Set the policy to enabled.
5. Set the "default for all apps" setting to one of the following values:

   1. User in control gives users control over the call history. They may allow or disallow apps access to the call history.
   2. Force Allow enables access to the Call History automatically. Users may not change this.
   3. Force Deny disables access to the Call History automatically. Users may not change this.

Windows Registry

1. Open the Windows Registry Editor.
2. Go to HKEY_LOCAL_MACHINE\Software\Policies\Microsoft\Windows\AppPrivacy
3. Right-click on AppPrivacy, and select New > Dword (32-bit) Value.
4. Name it LetAppsAccessCallHistory.
5. Give it one of the following values:

   1. A value of 0 means users are in control.
   2. A value of 1 means force allow.
   3. A value of 2 means force deny.

MDM policy from the Policy CSP (Privacy/LetAppsAccessCallHistory)

- A value of 0 means user is in control.
- A value of 1 means force allow.
- A value of 2 means force deny.

Email

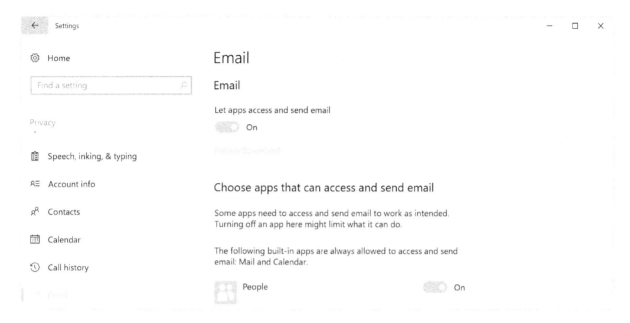

The Email privacy settings can be used to allow or disallow application access to emails on a global level, and to allow or disallow access for individual applications.

The two built-in applications Mail and Calendar are allowed to access and send email regardless of how the options are configured.

Let apps access and send email

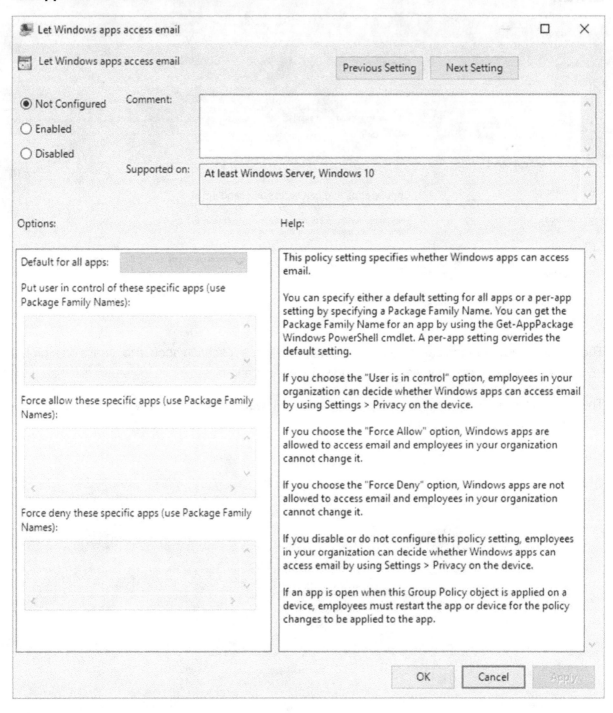

Let Windows apps access email		☐ ✕

Let Windows apps access email

Previous Setting | Next Setting

○ Not Configured
○ Enabled
○ Disabled

Comment:

Supported on: At least Windows Server, Windows 10

Options:

Default for all apps:

Put user in control of these specific apps (use Package Family Names):

Force allow these specific apps (use Package Family Names):

Force deny these specific apps (use Package Family Names):

Help:

This policy setting specifies whether Windows apps can access email.

You can specify either a default setting for all apps or a per-app setting by specifying a Package Family Name. You can get the Package Family Name for an app by using the Get-AppPackage Windows PowerShell cmdlet. A per-app setting overrides the default setting.

If you choose the "User is in control" option, employees in your organization can decide whether Windows apps can access email by using Settings > Privacy on the device.

If you choose the "Force Allow" option, Windows apps are allowed to access email and employees in your organization cannot change it.

If you choose the "Force Deny" option, Windows apps are not allowed to access email and employees in your organization cannot change it.

If you disable or do not configure this policy setting, employees in your organization can decide whether Windows apps can access email by using Settings > Privacy on the device.

If an app is open when this Group Policy object is applied on a device, employees must restart the app or device for the policy changes to be applied to the app.

OK | Cancel | Apply

Group Policy

This policy setting specifies whether Windows apps can access email.

You can specify either a default setting for all apps or a per-app setting by specifying a Package Family Name. You can get the Package Family Name for an app by using the Get-AppPackage Windows PowerShell cmdlet. A per-app setting overrides the default setting.

1. Open the Group Policy Editor.
2. Go to Computer Configuration > Administrative Templates > Windows Components > App Privacy
3. Select Let Windows apps access email
4. Set the policy to enabled.
5. Set the value of the policy under Default for apps:

    1. User is in control means that users can decide whether Windows apps may access email.
    2. Force Allow means that Windows apps are allowed to access email, and users cannot change it.
    3. Force Deny means that Windows apps are not allowed to access email, and that users cannot change it.

Windows Registry

1. Open the Windows Registry Editor.
2. Go to HKEY_LOCAL_MACHINE\Software\Policies\Microsoft\Windows\AppPrivacy
3. Right-click on AppPrivacy, and select New > Dword (32-bit) Value.
4. Name the new value LetAppsAccessEmail.

    1. Set its value to 0 to give users control over the feature.
    2. Set its value to 1 to force allow.
    3. Set its value to 2 to force deny.

MDM policy from the Policy CSP (Privacy/LetAppsAccessEmail)

1. 0 – user is in control.
2. 1 – Force allow
3. 2 – Force deny

Tasks

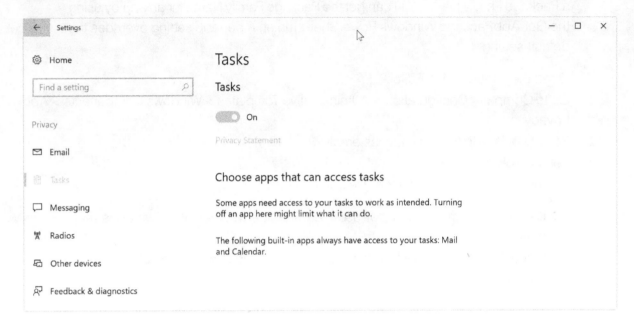

You may use the Tasks privacy page to allow or disallow global access to tasks, or to allow or disallow access to tasks for individual applications.

The two built-in applications Mail and Calendar are whitelisted. They have access to the tasks even if you disable tasks globally.

Group Policy

This policy setting specifies whether Windows apps can access tasks.

You can specify either a default setting for all apps or a per-app setting by specifying a Package Family Name. You can get the Package Family Name for an app by using the Get-AppPackage Windows PowerShell cmdlet. A per-app setting overrides the default setting.

1. Open the Group Policy Editor.
2. Go to Computer Configuration > Administrative Templates > Windows Components > App Privacy
3. Select Let Windows apps access Tasks
4. Set the policy to enabled.
5. Select one of the following values for "default for all apps".

   1. User is in control – Users may enable or disable Tasks access for all or specific apps.
   2. Force Allow – Tasks access is enabled, and users cannot change that.
   3. Force Deny – Tasks access is disabled, and users cannot change that.

Messaging

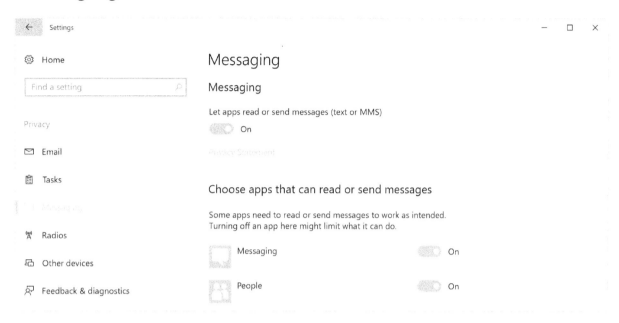

You may use the Messaging privacy options to turn on or off application read and send access to messages (both text and MMS).

It is furthermore possible to allow or disallow individual applications to use messaging.

Let apps read or send messages (text or MMS)

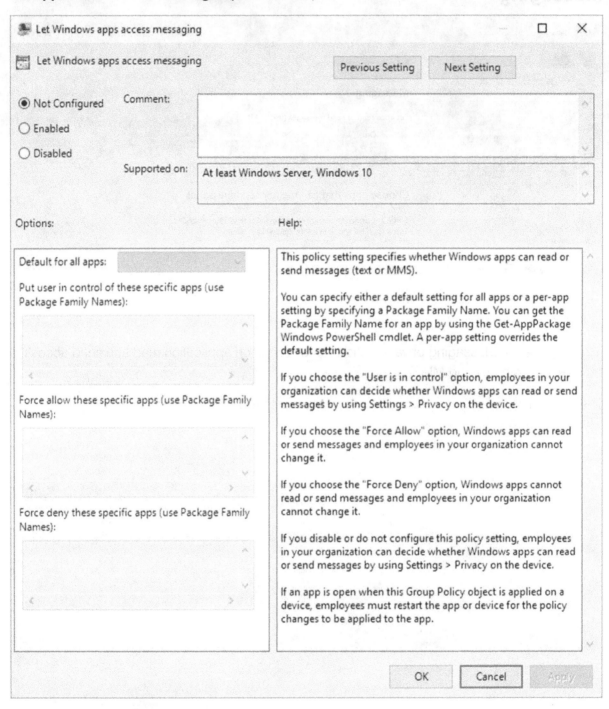

Group Policy

This policy setting specifies whether Windows apps can read or send messages (text or MMS).

You can specify either a default setting for all apps or a per-app setting by specifying a Package Family Name. You can get the Package Family Name for an app by using the Get-AppPackage Windows PowerShell cmdlet. A per-app setting overrides the default setting.

1. Open the Group Policy Editor.
2. Go to Computer Configuration > Administrative Templates > Windows Components > App Privacy
3. Select the Let Windows apps access messaging policy.
4. Set the policy to enabled.
5. Set the default for all apps value to

   1. User is in control to allow users to control the feature.
   2. Force Allow to enable app access to messaging, and block users from changing this.
   3. Force Deny to disallow app access to messaging, and block users from changing this.

Windows Registry

1. Open the Windows Registry Editor.
2. Go to HKEY_LOCAL_MACHINE\Software\Policies\Microsoft\Windows\AppPrivacy
3. Right-click on AppPrivacy, and select New > Dword (32-bit) Value.
4. Name it LetAppsAccessMessaging

   1. Set its value to 0 to put users in control.
   2. Set its value to 1 to force allow.
   3. Set its value to 2 to force deny.

MDM policy from the Policy CSP (Privacy/LetAppsAccessMessaging)

1. A value of 0 means user is in control.
2. A value of 1 means force allow
3. A value of 2 means force deny.

Radios

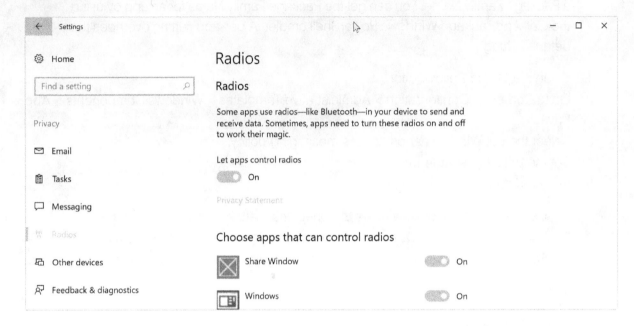

Some apps use radios – like Bluetooth – in your device to send and receive data. Sometimes, apps need to turn these radios on and off to work their magic.

You may use the Radios settings to allow or disallow access to Radios such as Bluetooth globally, or for individual applications.

Let Windows apps control radios

🪟 Let Windows apps control radios		□	✕

📷 Let Windows apps control radios

	Previous Setting	Next Setting

◉ Not Configured   Comment:

○ Enabled

○ Disabled

Supported on: At least Windows Server, Windows 10

Options:

Help:

Default for all apps:

Put user in control of these specific apps (use Package Family Names):

Force allow these specific apps (use Package Family Names):

Force deny these specific apps (use Package Family Names):

This policy setting specifies whether Windows apps have access to control radios.

You can specify either a default setting for all apps or a per-app setting by specifying a Package Family Name. You can get the Package Family Name for an app by using the Get-AppPackage Windows PowerShell cmdlet. A per-app setting overrides the default setting.

If you choose the "User is in control" option, employees in your organization can decide whether Windows apps have access to control radios by using Settings > Privacy on the device.

If you choose the "Force Allow" option, Windows apps will have access to control radios and employees in your organization cannot change it.

If you choose the "Force Deny" option, Windows apps will not have access to control radios and employees in your organization cannot change it.

If you disable or do not configure this policy setting, employees in your organization can decide whether Windows apps have access to control radios by using Settings > Privacy on the device.

If an app is open when this Group Policy object is applied on a device, employees must restart the app or device for the policy changes to be applied to the app.

OK	Cancel	Apply

Group Policy

This policy setting specifies whether Windows apps have access to control radios.

You can specify either a default setting for all apps or a per-app setting by specifying a Package Family Name. You can get the Package Family Name for an app by using the Get-AppPackage Windows PowerShell cmdlet. A per-app setting overrides the default setting.

1. Open the Group Policy Editor.
2. Go to Computer Configuration > Administrative Templates > Windows Components > App Privacy
3. Select Let Windows apps control radios.
4. Set the policy to enabled.
5. Set the default for all apps value to

   1. User is in control to let users decide.
   2. Force Allow to enable application access to control radios, and prevent users from changing that.
   3. Force Deny to disable application access to control radios, and prevent users from changing that.

Windows Registry

1. Open the Registry Editor
2. Go to HKEY_LOCAL_MACHINE\Software\Policies\Microsoft\Windows\AppPrivacy
3. Right-click on AppPrivacy, and select New > Dword (32-bit) Value.
4. Name it LetAppsAccessRadios.

   1. Set its value to 0 for user is in control.
   2. Set its value to 1 for force allow.
   3. Set its value to 2 for force deny.

MDM policy of the Policy CSP (Privacy/LetAppsAccessRadios)

1. A value of 0 means that the user is in control.
2. A value of 1 means force allow.
3. A value of 2 means force deny.

Other Devices

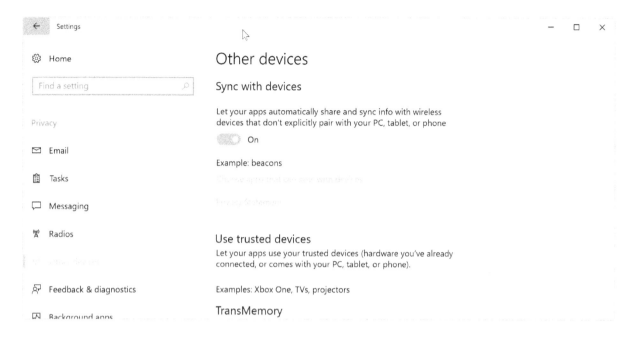

Manage other devices, those that you sync data with, or that you connect to your Windows machine using this setting. Other devices may be other Windows 10 devices but also tablets or phones.

Applications may use your trusted devices, such as your Xbox One, TVs, or projectors.

The following options are provided:

- Enable or disable the synchronization of data with other devices.
- Choose apps that can sync with the device you are using.
- Let applications uses Trusted Devices such as memory cards, Xbox and other devices.

Feedback & Diagnostics

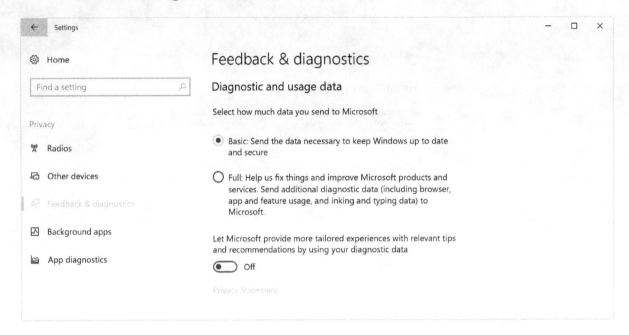

The Windows 10 Creators Update supports two diagnostic settings (down from three in previous versions of Windows.

The only exception to that is that Enterprise editions support turning off diagnostics completely.

Basic – See this Microsoft page for a full list of what is collected: https://docs.microsoft.com/en-us/windows/configuration/basic-level-windows-diagnostic-events-and-fields

> The Basic level gathers a limited set of information that is critical for understanding the device and its configuration including: basic device information, quality-related information, app compatibility, and Microsoft Store. When the level is set to Basic, it also includes the Security level information.

> The Basic level helps to identify problems that can occur on a particular device hardware or software configuration. For example, it can help determine if crashes are more frequent on devices with a specific amount of memory or that are running a particular driver version. This helps Microsoft fix operating system or app problems.

Full – includes all basic level data sets, and additional data sets. You find a listing of those here: https://docs.microsoft.com/en-us/windows/configuration/windows-diagnostic-data

Windows should ask for my feedback

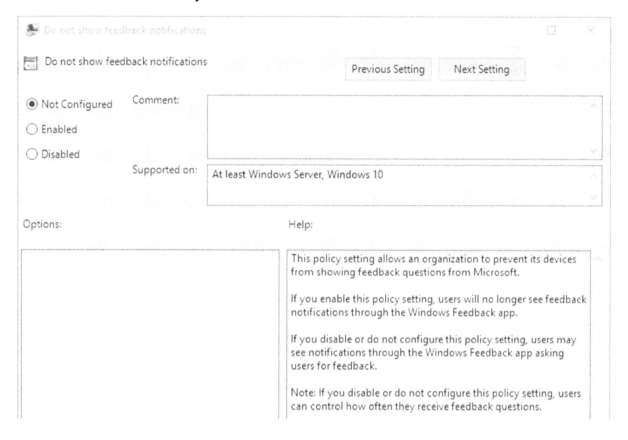

Group Policy

This policy setting allows an organization to prevent its devices from showing feedback questions from Microsoft.

1. Open the Group Policy Editor.
2. Go to Computer Configuration > Administrative Templates > Windows Components > Data Collection and Preview Builds
3. Select Do not show feedback notifications.

   1. Enable this policy to block feedback notifications through the Windows Feedback application.
   2. Disable this policy, or don't configure it, to allow feedback notifications through the Windows Feedback application.

Windows Registry

1. Open the Windows Registry Editor.
2. Go to HKEY_LOCAL_MACHINE\Software\Policies\Microsoft\Windows\DataCollection

3. Right-click on DataCollection, and select New > Dword (32-bit) Value.
4. Name it DoNotShowFeedbackNotifications

   1. A value of 1 disables feedback notifications.
   2. A value of 0 allows them.

Alternatively

1. Go to HKEY_CURRENT_USER\Software\Microsoft\Siuf\Rules\
2. Right-click on Rules, and select New > Dword (32-bit value)
3. Name it PeriodInNanoSeconds
4. Set its value according to the table below.
5. Go to HKEY_CURRENT_USER\Software\Microsoft\Siuf\Rules\
6. Right-click on Rules, and select New > Dword (32-bit value)
7. Name it NumberOfSIUFInPeriod
8. Set its value according to the table below

Setting	PeriodInNanoSeconds	NumberOfSIUFInPeriod
Automatically	Delete the registry setting	Delete the registry setting
Never	0	0
Always	100000000	Delete the registry setting
Once a day	864000000000	1
Once a week	6048000000000	1

Use Diagnostic Data for Tailored Experiences

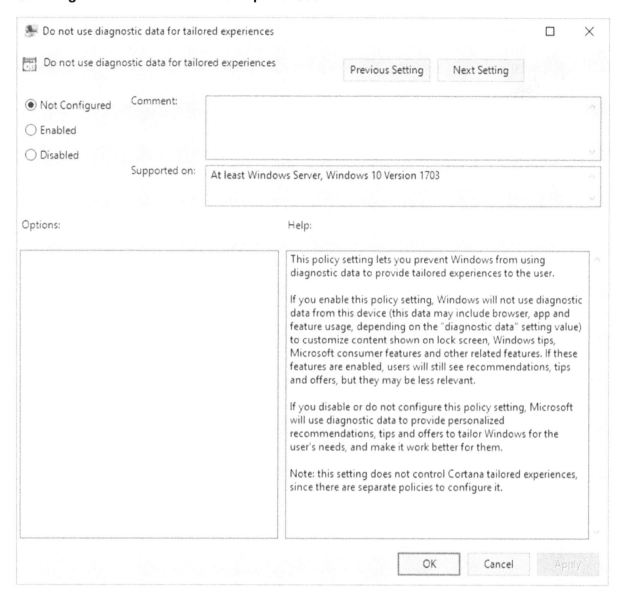

Group Policy

This policy setting lets you prevent Windows from using diagnostic data to provide tailored experiences to the user.

1. Open the Group Policy Editor
2. Go to User Configuration > Administrative Templates > Windows Components > Cloud Content

3. Select Do not use diagnostic data for tailored experiences.

    1. Set this policy to enabled if you don't want Windows to use diagnostic data from the device to customize content shown on the lock screen, and elsewhere.
    2. Set this policy to disabled, to enable personalized recommendations based on telemetry data.

Background Apps

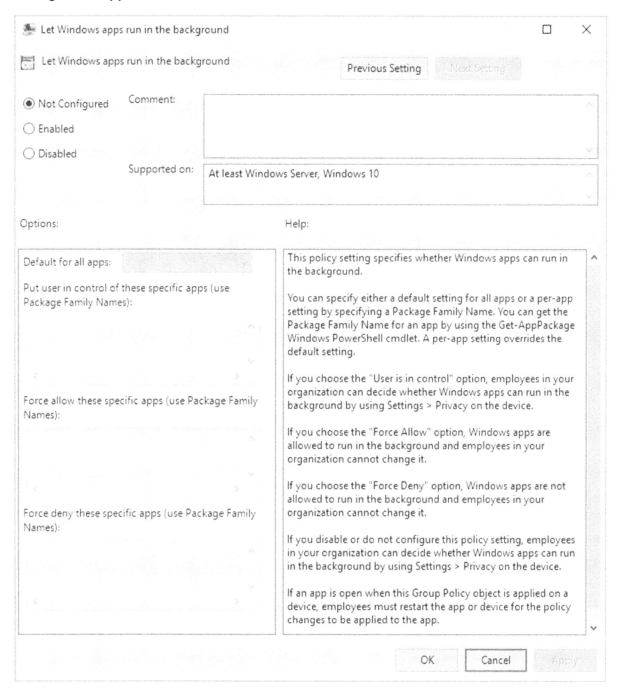

Applications may run in the background, for instance to receive information from the Internet or a network, or send notifications.

If you turn off the feature, apps may not do so when they are not running on the system. A positive side effect of turning the functionality off is that you may conserve power depending on which apps are installed on the system, and how they are used.

The Settings application provides you with two options:

1. Turn of the feature for all applications.
2. Select the apps that you want to be able to run in the background.

Group Policy

This policy setting specifies whether Windows apps can run in the background.

You can specify either a default setting for all apps or a per-app setting by specifying a Package Family Name. You can get the Package Family Name for an app by using the Get-AppPackage Windows PowerShell cmdlet. A per-app setting overrides the default setting.

1. Open the Group Policy Editor.
2. Go to Computer Configuration > Administrative Templates > Windows Components > App Privacy
3. Select Let Windows apps run in the background.
4. Set the policy to enabled.
5. Set one of the following options under "default for all apps"

   1. User is in control to provide users with options to enable or disable the functionality.
   2. Force Allow to allow apps to run in the background; users cannot change the preference.
   3. Force Deny to disallow apps to run in the background; users cannot change the preference.

Windows Registry

1. Open the Windows Registry Editor.
2. Go to HKEY_CURRENT_USER\Software\Microsoft\Windows\CurrentVersion\Background AccessApplications
3. Right-click on BackgroundAccessApplications, and select New > Dword (32-bit) Value.
4. Name it GlobalUserDisabled.

   1. A value of 0 means the feature is turned on.
   2. A value of 1 means the feature is disabled.

Let Windows and your apps use your motion data and collect motion history

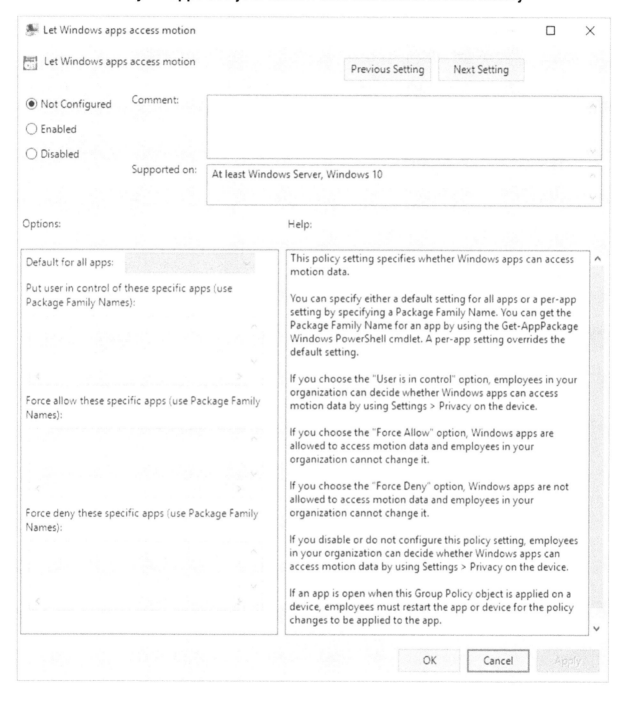

Windows applications may access motion data and collect the motion history. This requires special sensors in the device.

This policy setting specifies whether Windows apps can access motion data.

You can specify either a default setting for all apps or a per-app setting by specifying a Package Family Name. You can get the Package Family Name for an app by using the Get-AppPackage Windows PowerShell cmdlet. A per-app setting overrides the default setting.

Group Policy: Computer Configuration > Administrative Templates > Windows Components > App Privacy > Let Windows apps access motion

- Enabled – Default value. Windows apps may use motion data and collect motion history. Set Default for all apps value:

    ° User is in control – Users may enable or disable Motion in the Settings.
    ° Force allow – Motion is enabled, and users may not change that.
    ° Force deny – Motion is disabled, and users may not change that either.

- Disabled – Windows applications may not use motion data or collect motion history.

Key: HKEY_LOCAL_MACHINE\SOFTWARE\Policies\Microsoft\Windows\AppPrivacy

Name: LetAppsAccessMotion

Type: Dword

- A value of 0 means that the user is in control.
- A value of 1 means force allow.
- A value of 2 means force deny.

Windows Features

Accounts (Local, Microsoft)

Windows 10 supports two types of accounts: local accounts and Microsoft accounts. Microsoft prioritizes Microsoft accounts on Windows 10, but users may select to create local accounts instead.

The choice that users make during installation or setup, has a big impact on privacy and functionality.

Microsoft account vs local accounts

A Microsoft account is a relatively new top-level account for Microsoft software and service users. The best way to describe it is that it is an online account for all things Microsoft. Instead of having to sign up for different Microsoft products and services individually, you may use a Microsoft account for the majority of those.

Many Windows users may have access to a Microsoft account already. This is the case for instance when they use one of Microsoft's email services, for instance Outlook.com.

It needs to be noted that Microsoft accounts don't have a single domain they are associated with. In fact, it is possible to use any email address to set up a Microsoft account.

The easiest way to distinguish local from Microsoft accounts is that Microsoft accounts always use an email address as the username.

The use of a Microsoft account on Windows 10 comes with certain benefits:

Data synchronization – Some operating system preferences, customization, and some data is synced automatically to any device that runs Windows 10 provided that you sign in with the same Microsoft Account. This includes the theme and desktop wallpaper, Internet Explorer settings, the Edge browsing history, saved passwords, and Ease of Access. Check out the OneDrive / File Synchronization chapter for additional information on that.

- **Password reset and change** – Since a Microsoft account is an online account, you may go online to reset the account password, or change the password.

- **Direct access to apps and services** – Other apps and services that run on a Windows 10 machine may pick up the Microsoft account automatically so that you don't need to create an account, or sign in to one. OneDrive may sign you in to your online storage, or you may see your emails or contacts listed directly in the apps that provide the information.

- **Multi-device access** – You can sign in to any Windows 10 device using a Microsoft account, while you would need to create local accounts on any device you want to use if you use local accounts.

- **Windows Store** – Windows Store restricts access to non-Microsoft accounts: Windows 10 Pro, Enterprise and Education editions support the downloading of free apps and games from the store. A Microsoft is required on Home editions, and for any purchases made in the Store.

The core benefit of using a local account is privacy. Microsoft account data is submitted to Microsoft by default, and stored on company servers.

Microsoft's privacy statement confirms as much:

> *Microsoft collects data to operate effectively and provide you the best experiences with our products. You provide some of this data directly, such as when you create a Microsoft account, submit a search query to Bing, speak a voice command to Cortana, upload a document to OneDrive, purchase an MSDN subscription, sign up for Office 365, or contact us for support.*[15]

Please note that you may limit the data that is shared with Microsoft by customizing Windows 10 settings as described in this book.

Other differences exist: you cannot change a Microsoft account password on the local Windows 10 machine, as Internet access is required for that. The same is not true for changing the password of a local account, as you can do so directly on the local machine, even without Internet access.

---

[15] https://privacy.microsoft.com/en-us/privacystatement

Windows Setup with a local account

Microsoft puts the focus on Microsoft accounts during setup. It displays the "sign in with Microsoft" option during setup, and gives customers the option to sign in using an existing account, or to create a new account.

The local account option is still there, but it is not highlighted as much. The following guide walks you through the steps of setting up a local account on a Windows 10 machine during setup.

Step 1: Select Offline account on the "Sign in with Microsoft" page during setup.

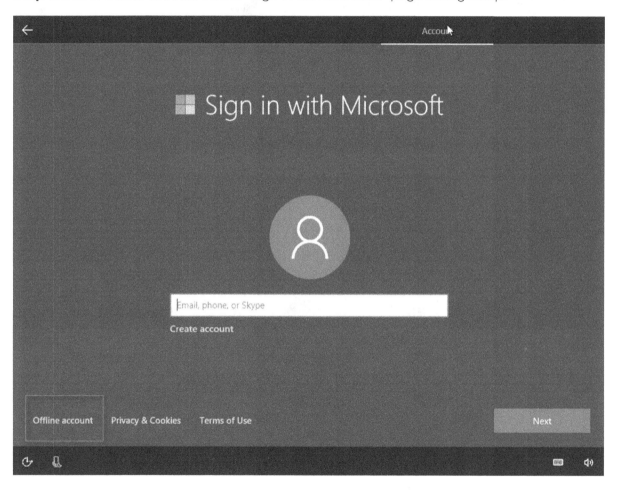

Step 2: Select No or Later on the next screen. Microsoft tries one more time on this page to get you to sign up or in using a Microsoft account.

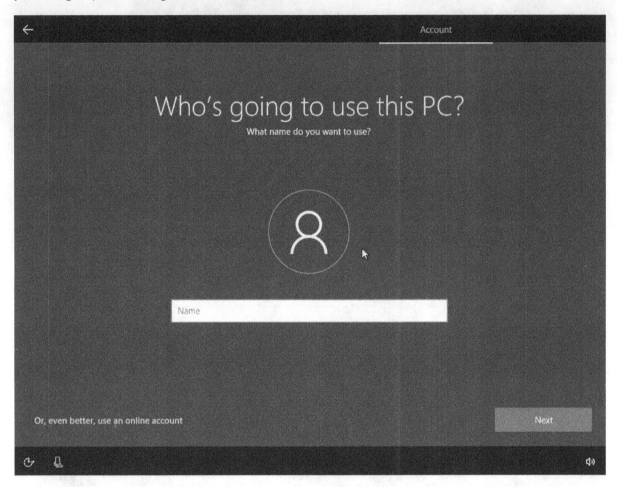

Step 3: Select a username for the local account, and click on the Next button afterwards.

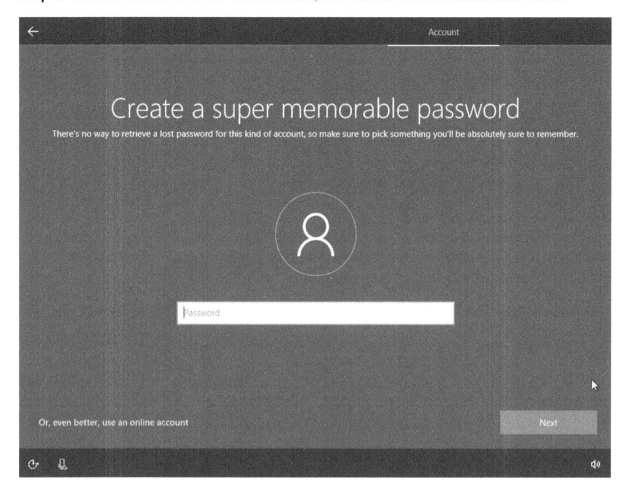

Step 4: Type a password, or leave the password field empty, and click on next.

That's it; you have created a local account during setup which you can use from that moment on to sign in to the device.

Convert a Microsoft account login to a local account (or vice versa)

You have two options when it comes to switching from a local account to a Microsoft account, or a Microsoft account to a local account.

Conversion is useful if you have selected either account type during setup, and want to switch to the other.

While you can create a new user account on the device and make it the preferred account type, you may also convert an existing account type into the other. Converting offers advantages over the creation of new user accounts on the device.,

Note that converting to the other account type does not change files or installed applications on the device. Access remains, and that is the main difference to creating a new user account on the device for use as a local or Microsoft account.

You may be asked to sign in to apps that require a Microsoft account when you switch to a local account though.

Switch from a local account to a Microsoft account

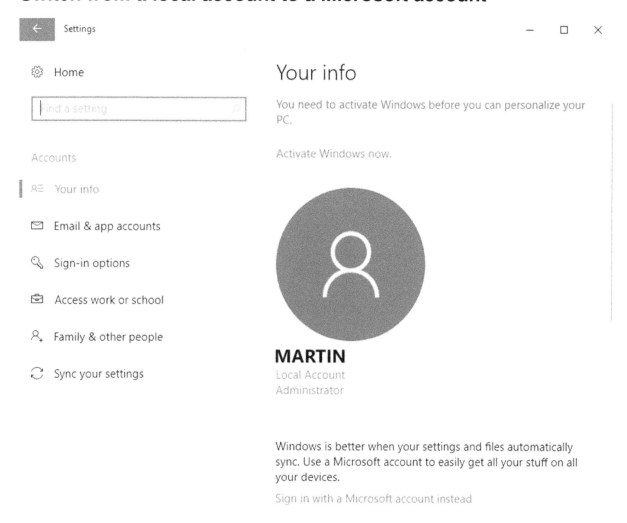

Start by opening the Settings application. Go to Accounts > Your Info.

The page lists the account type, e.g. local account as you see on the screenshot above, and a link to "sign in with a Microsoft account instead".

A click on the link starts the conversion process from using a local account to using a Microsoft account.

You are asked to authenticate by entering the Microsoft account email address, phone number associated with a Microsoft account, or a Skype ID.

Once you complete the authentication process, you are asked to enter the password of the local Windows account to complete the process.

The next time you sign in to the Windows 10 device, you are asked to enter the Microsoft account password and not the local password.

Switch from a Microsoft account to a local account

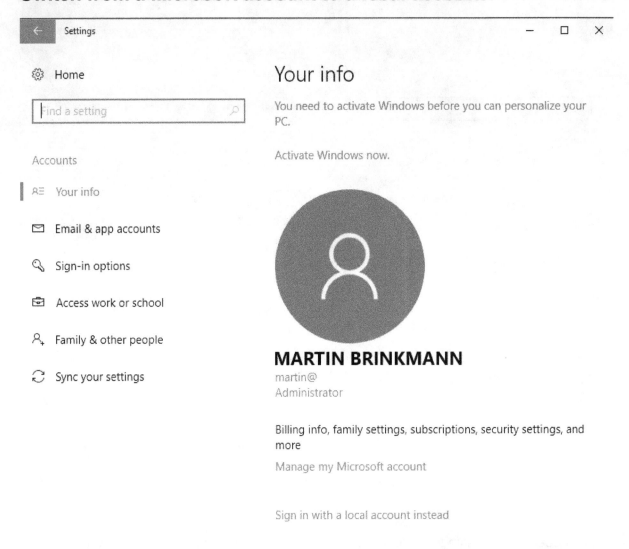

You may switch from a Microsoft account to a local account as well. The process is nearly identical to switching from a local account to a Microsoft account.

Start by opening the Settings application. Go to Accounts > Your Info.

If you see an email address listed on the page that opens, you are signed in using a Microsoft account.

Scroll down until you find the "sign in with a local account instead" link, and activate it.

First thing you are asked to do is enter the current Microsoft account password.

Once you have done that, you create a new local account by selecting a username, password and password hint. Note that the user name is the only mandatory field.

When you sign in the next time, you are asked to enter the local account password for authentication.

Use a Microsoft account in select applications

Windows 10 users who sign in with a local account may notice that some functionality that applications provide may become unavailable because of that.

This is the case usually for any application that is linked to a Microsoft Account. OneDrive for instance requires a Microsoft account, and so do other applications such as Calendar or Music. Other applications may function partially only.

Windows Store works with a local account if you run Windows 10 Pro or Enterprise for instance, but only to download and install free apps.

A rule of thumb is that Windows apps will notify you when they need access to a Microsoft account.

You do need to be careful however when you sign in to a Microsoft account this way. Microsoft displays an authentication prompt to use the Microsoft account for this particular application.

The next screen displays an option to switch to a Microsoft account when signing in. If you want to keep on using your local account, you need to click on the link that is displayed beneath the password field to use the Microsoft account only for the selected application and not Windows in general.

Manage the data that Microsoft associates with a Microsoft account

Microsoft created a management interface for Microsoft account on the official company website. It provides users with options to manage user information, privacy, and security online.

The main entry points are:

Your Info: https://account.microsoft.com/profile/

Privacy: https://account.microsoft.com/privacy/

Security: https://account.microsoft.com/security

Your Info

Your Info lists profile and contact information, and options to modify those. You may use the page to manage your sign-in email addresses and phone numbers, edit personal or billing information, and to change the account picture.

Privacy

The Privacy tab on the Microsoft account website lists some of the data that Microsoft collects when you use Windows 10 or company services.

Browse

Users who sign in to Windows 10, use Cortana's browsing history feature, and use Microsoft Edge, have their browsing history sent to Microsoft so that Microsoft, apps and Windows features may provide "timely and intelligent answers and proactive personalized suggestions".

Tip: Windows 10 users may disable the transferal of the browsing history by opening Cortana, selecting Notebook > Permissions, and setting the Browsing History option to off.

Search

Bing uses a user's search history to improve results, personalization and suggestions. Cortana may use the search history as well to provide services.

Location

Microsoft services such as Maps use location data to show users where they are, and what is nearby. It may also be used to provide directions, and by other applications that ship with Windows 10 to provide certain functionality.

Cortana's Notebook

The digital agent Cortana keeps track of interests when it is active on a Windows 10 device. The notebook lists interests associated with the Microsoft account and sorted into categories such as News, Shopping, or Weather.

Tip: Select Notebook > Connected Services when Cortana is open to manage third-party services that Cortana may share information with.

The following options are provided at the time of writing:

- Manage the browsing history. Microsoft displays the most recent browsing history data, and options to clear it.
- Manage the search history. This lists recent searches, and options to clear the search history.
- Manage the location history. You may list the location history, and clear it on the page.
- Manage Cortana Notebook data. List the data that Cortana associates with your interests, and delete the data.

Security

The Security tab lists options to change the account password, update security information, and to view the recent activity.

You may check and update security information there. This is important as Microsoft will use the information you provide for account recovery operations.

The "review recent activity" option lists the last sign-ins to the account, and from where they happened. Useful to make sure all are legit.

Customer Experience Program

Turn off Windows Customer Experience Improvement Program

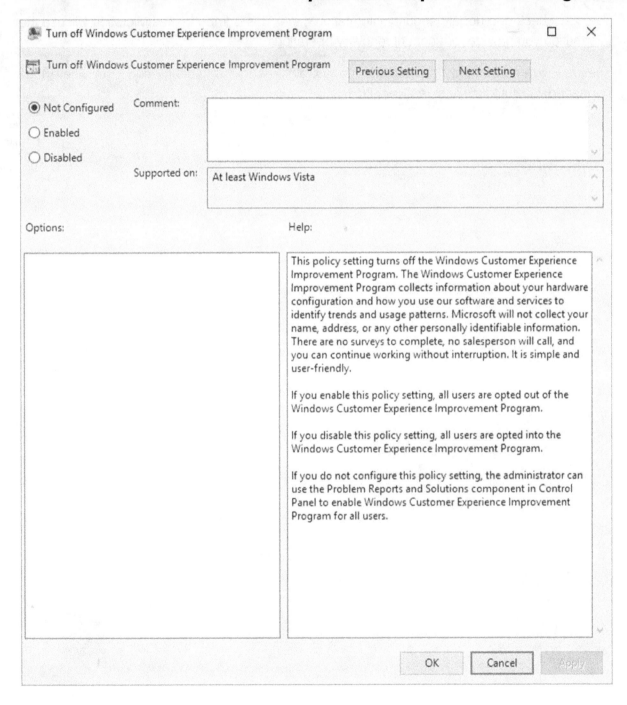

The program collects information about the hardware configuration, and software and services use, to identify trends and usage patterns.

Microsoft states that it won't collect personally identifiable information such as names or addresses.

Group Policy:

Computer Configuration > Administrative Templates > System > Internet Communication Management > Internet Communication settings > Turn off Windows Customer Experience Improvement Program

- Enabled – When enabled, all users are opted out of the Windows Customer Experience Improvement Program.
- Disabled – All users are opted in to the Windows Customer Experience Improvement Program.

Windows Registry:

Key: HKEY_LOCAL_MACHINE\SOFTWARE\Policies\Microsoft\SQMClient\Windows

Name: CEIPEnable

Type: Dword

- 0 – The feature is disabled.
- 1 – The feature is enabled.

Allow Corporate Redirection of Customer Experience Improvement uploads

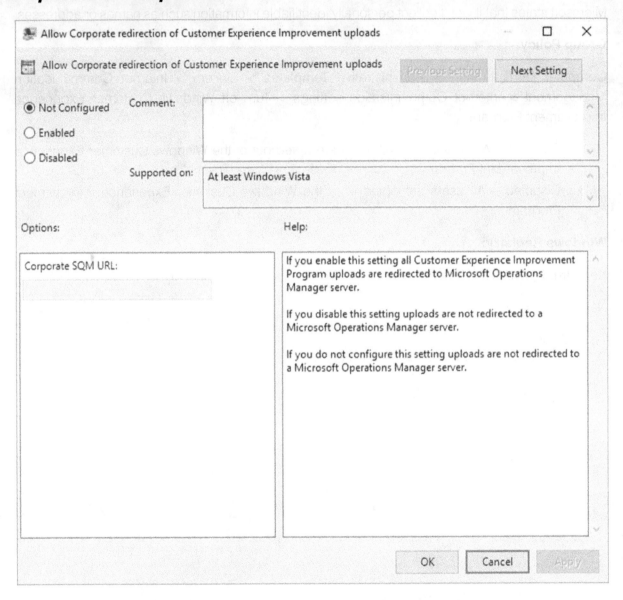

This setting allows you to change the resource the collected data gets uploaded to.

Policy: Computer Configuration > Administrative Templates > Windows Components > Windows Customer Experience Improvement Program > Allow Corporate Redirection of Customer Experience Improvement uploads

- Enabled – This redirects all Customer Experience Improvement uploads to the selected address.
- Disabled – Uploads are not redirected by go to the default address.

Key: HKEY_LOCAL_MACHINE\SOFTWARE\Policies\Microsoft\SQMClient

Name: CorporateSQMURL

Type: String

- Set new resource address, or redirect to localhost 127.0.0.1

Turn off the Windows Messenger Customer Experience Improvement Program

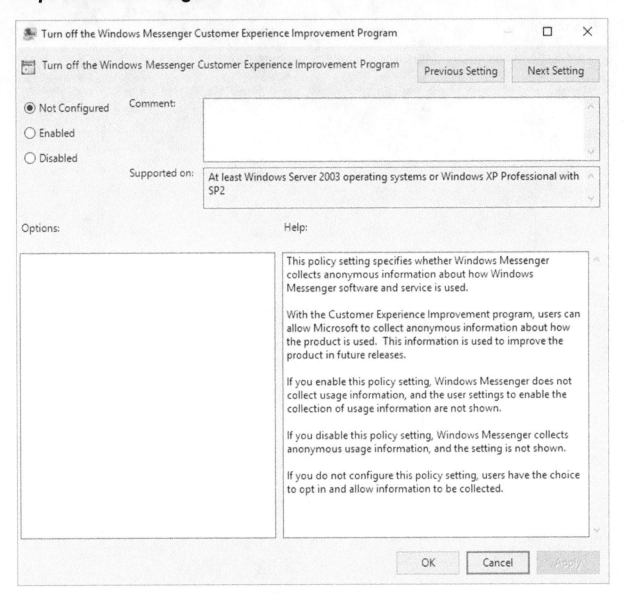

This setting defines whether Windows Messenger collects anonymous information about how Windows Messenger is used on the system.

Policy: Computer Configuration > Administrative Templates > System > Internet Communication Management > Internet Communication settings > Turn off the Windows Messenger Customer Experience Improvement Program

- Enabled – Windows Messenger does not collect usage information about how the product is used.

- Disabled – Anonymous Windows Messenger usage data is collected and submitted to Microsoft

Key: HKEY_LOCAL_MACHINE\SOFTWARE\Policies\Microsoft\Messenger\Client

Name: CEIP

Type: Dword

- 2 – Anonymous usage data is not collected.

Turn off Help Experience Improvement Program

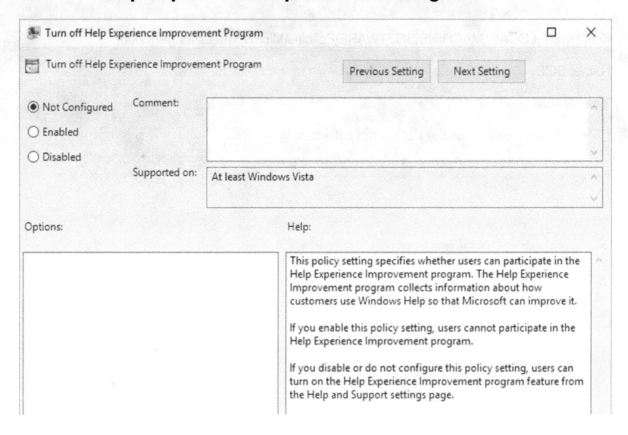

This policy determines whether users may participate in the Help Experience Improvement program. The program collects information on how users use Windows Help.

Group Policy:

User Configuration > Administrative Templates > System > Internet Communication Management > Internet Communication settings > Turn off Help Experience Improvement Program

- Enabled – Users cannot participate in the Help Experience Improvement Program.
- Disabled – Same as not configured. Users can turn the feature on.

Windows Registry:

Key: HKEY_CURRENT_USER\Software\Policies\Microsoft\Assistance\Client\1.0

Name: NoExplicitFeedback

Type: Dword

- 0 – Explicit Feedback is turned off.
- 1 – Explicit Feedback is turned on.

Name: NoImplicitFeedback

Type: Dword

- 0 – Implicit Feedback is turned off.
- 1 – Implicit Feedback is turned on.

Windows Media Player Usage Tracking

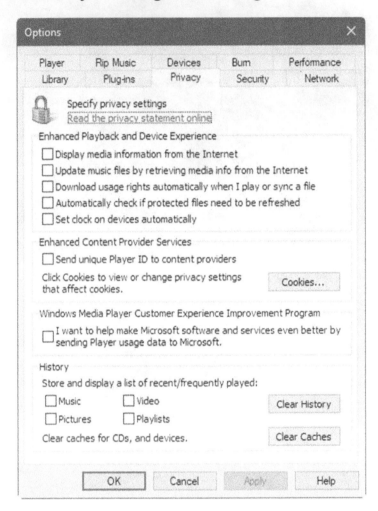

Windows Media Player Settings:

- Open Windows Media Player, and select Tools > Options > Privacy.
- Find the preference "I want to help make Microsoft software and services even better by sending Player usage data to Microsoft" and make sure it is disabled.

Windows Registry:

Key: HKEY_CURRENT_USER\ Software\ Microsoft\ MediaPlayer\ Preferences

Name: UsageTracking

Type: Dword

- 0 – The Window Media Player Customer Experience Improvement Program is disabled.
- 1 – The Window Media Player Customer Experience Improvement Program is enabled.

Turn off Microsoft Consumer Experiences

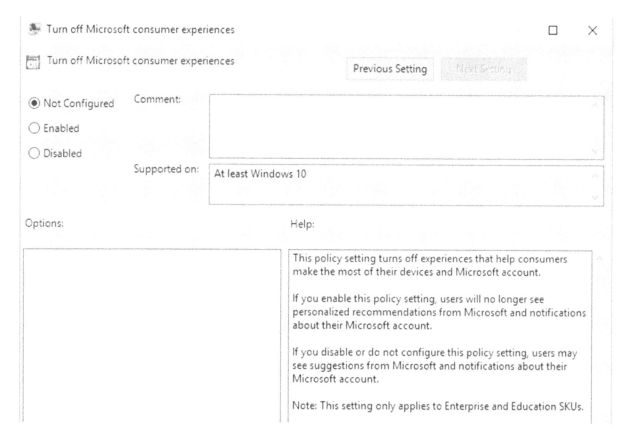

Microsoft Consumer Experiences were added to Windows 10 in version 1511. The feature powers several things on the device, including which third-party applications are shown on Start after installation or upgrade of a computer system, and personalized recommendations and notifications.

The policy applies only to Enterprise and Education versions of Windows 10.

Group Policy:

Computer Configuration > Administrative Templates > Windows Components > Cloud Content > Turn off Microsoft Consumer Experiences.

- Enabled: Microsoft Consumer Experiences is disabled if you enable the policy. If you disable the feature, Windows 10 won't push third-party application suggestions anymore on the system. It will also block recommendations and notifications that Microsoft Consumer Experiences powers as well.
- Disabled: Same as not configured. Microsoft Consumer Experiences is enabled.

Windows Registry:

Key: HKEY_LOCAL_MACHINE\SOFTWARE\Policies\Microsoft\Windows\CloudContent

Name: DisableWindowsConsumerFeatures

Type: Dword

- 0 – The feature is active on the system.
- 1 – The feature is disabled.

Feedback and Help

Turn off Active Help

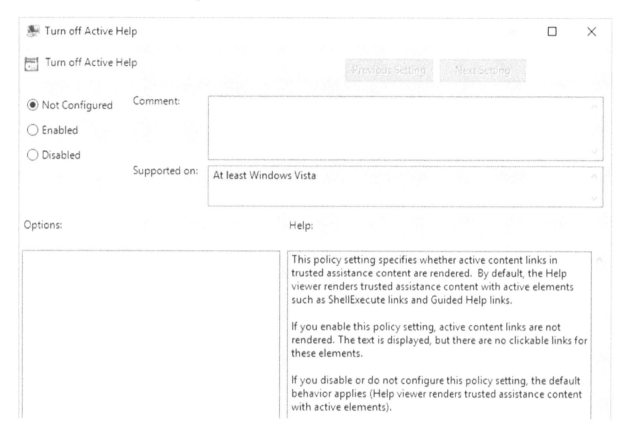

This setting defines whether so-called active content links are rendered in trusted assistance content.

Group Policy

Computer Configuration > Administrative Templates > Windows Components > Online Assistance > Turn off Active Help

- Enabled – Active Content links are not rendered if you enable the policy setting. While the text is still displayed, links are not displayed.
- Disabled – Default behavior applies.

Windows Registry

Key: HKEY_LOCAL_MACHINE\SOFTWARE\Policies\Microsoft\Assistance\Client\1.0

Name: NoActiveHelp

Type: Dword

- 1 – This turns off the Active Help feature.
- 0 – Same as no setting. Active Help is enabled.

Internet Explorer

Windows 10 comes with Internet Explorer 11, but it is no longer the default web browser on machines running the operating system.

Allow Microsoft services to provide enhanced suggestions as the user types in the Address bar

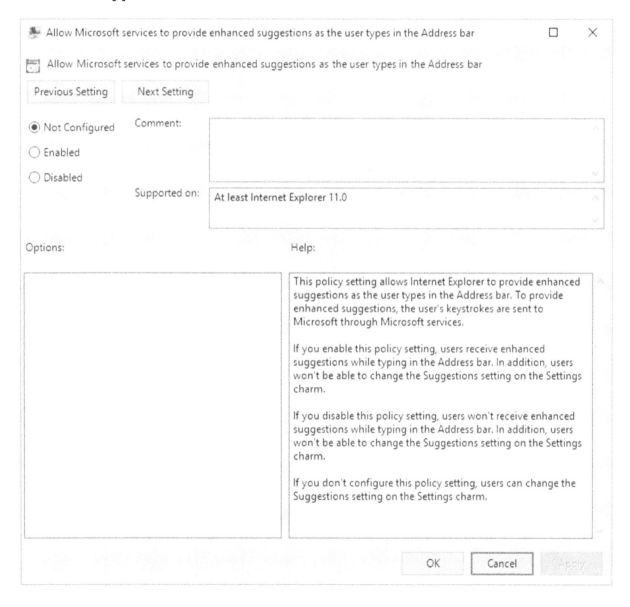

Microsoft's Internet Explorer may display suggestions based on the user's input. Enhanced suggestions are returned when the keystrokes are sent to Microsoft.

Group Policy

Computer Configuration > Administrative Templates > Windows Components > Internet Explorer > Allow Microsoft services to provide enhanced suggestions as the user types in the Address bar

- Enabled – Users will get enhanced suggestions when they type in Internet Explorer's address bar. This means that the keystrokes are sent to Microsoft. Users may not change the setting.
- Disabled – Enhanced suggestions are turned off. Users may not change the setting.
- Not Configured – Users are allowed to change the setting.

Windows Registry

Key: HKEY_LOCAL_MACHINE\SOFTWARE\Policies\Microsoft

Name: AllowServicePoweredQSA

Type: Dword

- 0 – Enhanced Suggestions are turned off in Internet Explorer.
- 1 – Enhanced Suggestions are enabled in the web browser.

Turn on Suggested Sites

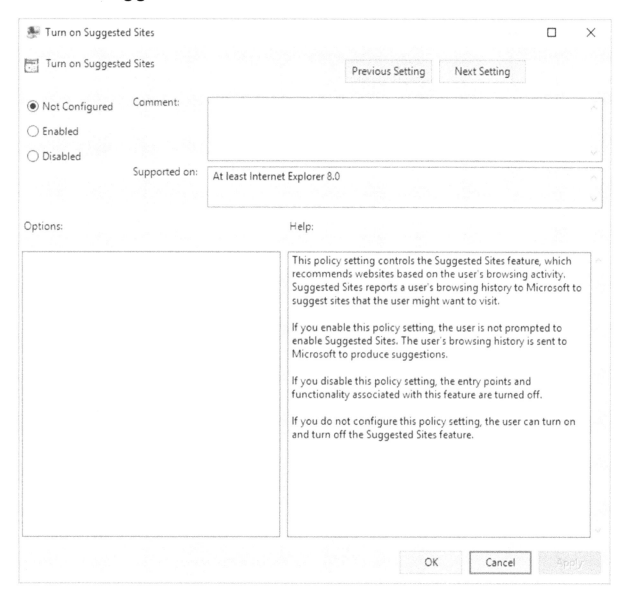

Microsoft Internet Explorer may display site suggestions based on the user's browsing history. If the feature is turned on, a user's browsing history is submitted to Microsoft.

Internet Options:

Open Microsoft Internet Explorer, and click on Menu > Internet Options.

Switch to the Advanced tab when the Internet Options window opens, and control "enable suggested sites" under Browsing on the page.

Group Policy:

- Computer Configuration > Administrative Templates > Windows Components > Internet Explorer > Turn on Suggested Sites Enabled – The feature is enabled, and users are not prompted to enable Suggested Sites. The browsing history is sent to Microsoft.
- Disabled – The Suggested Sites feature is turned off, and cannot be turned on by the user.
- Not configured – The user may turn the feature on or off.

Windows Registry:

Key: HKLM\Software\Policies\Microsoft\Internet Explorer\Suggested Sites

Name: Enabled

Type: Dword

- 0 – Suggested Sites is disabled.
- 1 – Suggested Sites is enabled.

Turn off URL Suggestions

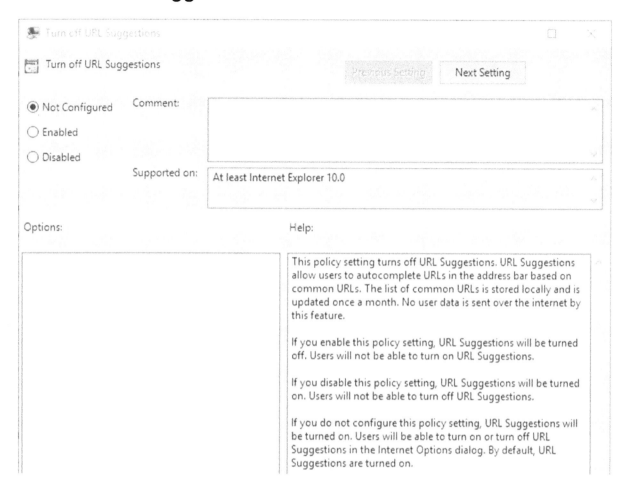

Microsoft's Internet Explorer displays suggestions based on what the user types in the browser's address bar. Internet Explorer uses a locally stored list for the autocomplete feature. User data is not sent over the Internet when the feature is enabled.

Internet Options:

Open Microsoft Internet Explorer, and click on Menu > Internet Options.

Select Content > Settings (next to AutoComplete). Remove "suggesting URLs" from the list of sources that Internet Explorer uses for the feature.

Group Policy:

Computer Configuration > Administrative Templates > Windows Components > Internet Explorer > Internet Settings > AutoComplete > Turn off URL Suggestions

- Enabled – URL suggestions are disabled. Users cannot enable the feature.

- Disabled – URL suggestions are enabled, and users may not turn the feature off.
- Not Configured – Users may enable or disable the feature.

Windows Registry

Key: HKEY_CURRENT_USER\Software\Microsoft\Windows\CurrentVersion\Explorer\AutoComplete

Name: Append Completion

Type: String Value

- yes – Internet Explorer tries to match what the user types with the locally stored autocomplete listing.
- no – URL suggestions are disabled in Internet Explorer.

Turn off Windows Search AutoComplete

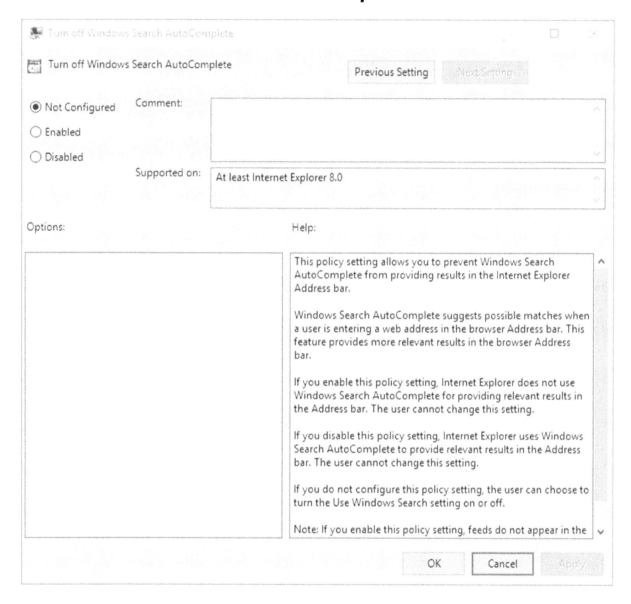

This determines whether Windows Search may provide autocomplete results when users type in the Internet Explorer address bar.

Internet Options:

Open Microsoft Internet Explorer, and click on Menu > Internet Options.

Select Content > Settings (next to AutoComplete). Remove "Use Windows Search for better results" from the list of sources that Internet Explorer uses for the feature.

Group Policy:

Computer Configuration > Administrative Templates > Windows Components > Internet Explorer > Internet Settings > AutoComplete > Turn off Windows Search AutoComplete

- Enabled – If you enable this policy, Internet Explorer won't use Windows Search for providing results in the address bar. Users won't be able to change the setting.
- Disabled – Internet Explorer uses Windows Search to provide results in the browser's address bar. Users may not change the setting.
- Not Configured – Users may turn the feature on or off. The feature is enabled by default.

Windows Registry:

Key: HKEY_CURRENT_USER\Software\Microsoft\Internet Explorer\Main\WindowsSearch\

Name: AutoCompleteGroups

Type: Dword

- 0 – Disable the use of Windows Search for AutoComplete functionality.

Microsoft Edge

Microsoft Edge is the default system browser of Windows 10. It is not the only browser that ships with Windows 10, as Internet Explorer 11 is available as well.

The main reason why Microsoft made the decision to include Edge and IE in Windows 10 is backwards compatibility.

Microsoft Edge was designed to be a lightweight browser that supports major web standards. It comes without features such a support for ActiveX or Browser Helper Objects which Internet Explorer continues to support.

Allow Address bar drop-down list suggestions

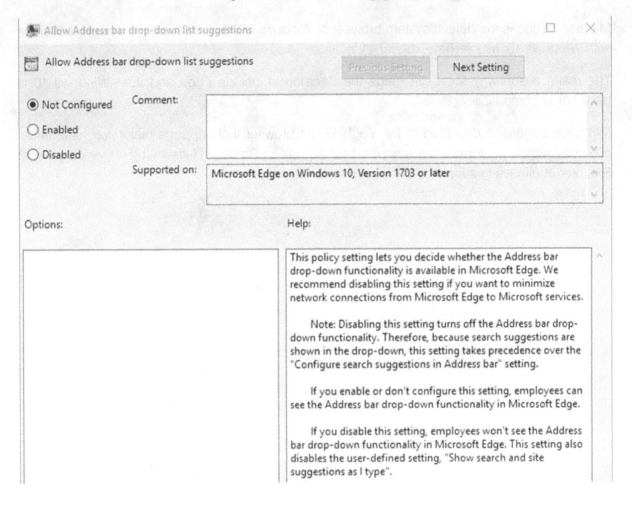

Microsoft Edge may display suggestions in the Address bar drop-down menu when users start to type. This particular setting disables the whole drop-down menu.

If you don't want search results displayed only, you may leave this setting alone and configure "Configure search suggestions in Address bar instead".

Group Policy

Computer Configuration > Administrative Templates > Windows Components > Microsoft Edge > Allow Address bar drop-down list suggestions

- Enabled – Same as not configured. Address bar drop-down functionality is enabled in Microsoft Edge. Microsoft Edge may connect to Microsoft services for the functionality if the setting is enabled.
- Disabled – Drop-down suggestions are disabled. Setting this policy to disabled, disables "show search and site suggestions as I type" as well.

Allow Microsoft Compatibility List

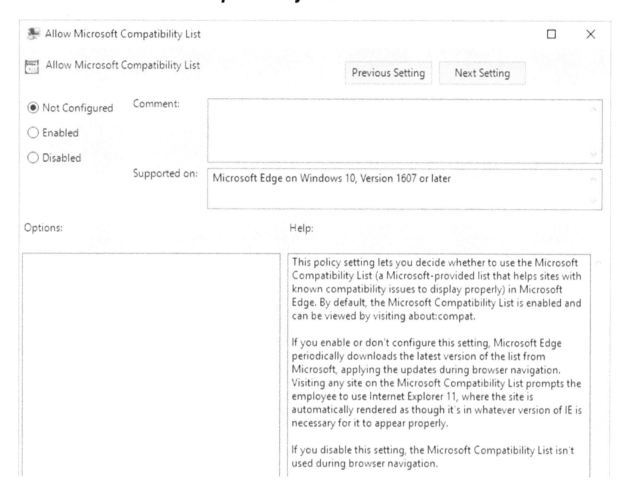

Microsoft maintains a list of sites with known compatibility issues in Microsoft Edge. Edge prompts users to open sites that are on the list in Internet Explorer instead. This is done so that these sites, usually sites optimized for a particular version of Internet Explorer, correctly.

The Microsoft Compatibility List is enabled by default and Windows 10 will check for updates of the list frequently.

Policy: Computer Configuration > Administrative Templates > Windows Components > Microsoft Edge > Allow Microsoft Compatibility List

- Enabled – Same as not configured. Microsoft Edge downloads an updated compatibility list periodically.
- Disabled – The Microsoft Compatibility List is not used.

Allow web content on New Tab page

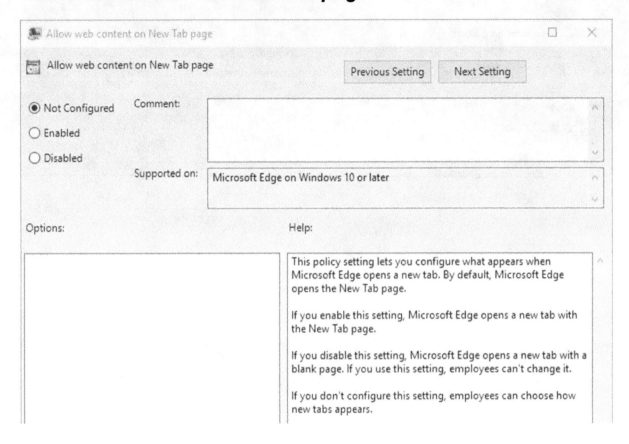

The policy lets you configure the content of the New Tab page in Microsoft Edge. Microsoft Edge displays top sites and content such as news that it pulls from the Internet on the New Tab page by default.

Policy: Computer Configuration > Administrative Templates > Windows Components > Microsoft Edge > Allow web content on New Tab page

- Enabled – Microsoft Edge displays the default New Tab page of the web browser.
- Disabled – Microsoft Edge displays a blank New Tab page without any content.
- Not configured – Users may choose what appears on the New Tab page.

Configure Cookies

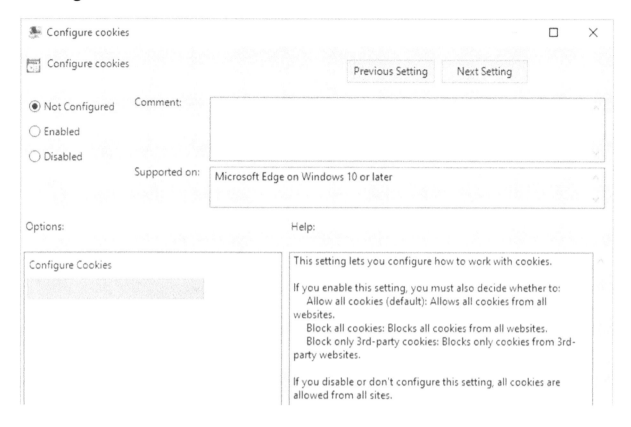

Edge users may configure how cookies are handled by the browser directly in Edge. A policy is available to configure cookie behavior for all users of a machine.

Microsoft Edge Settings:

- Open Microsoft Edge.
- Select Menu (the three dots), and Settings from the menu.
- Scroll down and click on "view advanced settings".
- Locate the cookies section by scrolling down. You have three options when it comes to configuring the behavior:

  ° Block all cookies
  ° Block only third-party cookies
  ° Don't block cookies (default)

Group Policy:

Computer Configuration > Administrative Templates > Windows Components > Microsoft Edge > Configure cookies

- Enabled – When you enable this setting, you may use the policy to configure the cookie behavior of the Edge web browser. You may set it to the following:

    ○ Allow all cookies – This is the default behavior of Microsoft Edge. All cookies are allowed.
    ○ Block all cookies – You may block any cookie from being set in Edge.
    ○ Block only 3rd-party cookies – This allows first-party cookies, but blocks all third-party cookies in the browser.

- Disabled – Same as not configured. All cookies are allowed.

Configure Do Not Track

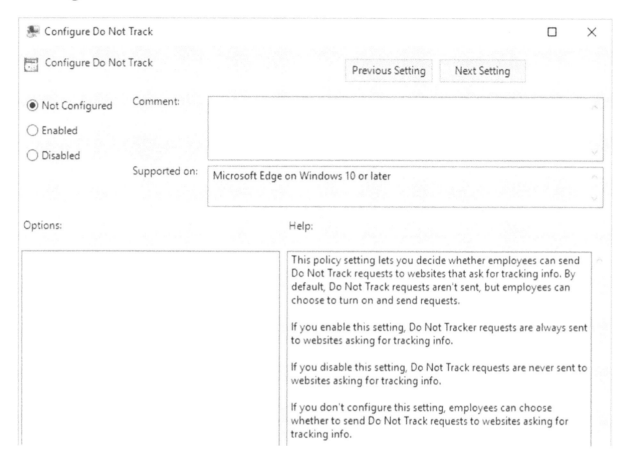

Microsoft Edge does not send Do Not Track requests by default. This setting lets you enable Do Not Track in Microsoft Edge, or give users the choice to do so.

Policy: Computer Configuration > Administrative Templates > Windows Components > Microsoft Edge > Configure Do Not Track

- Enabled – Do Not Track is enabled, and Edge sends the header information when it connects to websites.
- Disabled – Do Not Track is disabled.
- Not configured – Users may enable or disable Do Not Track.

Configure search suggestions in Address bar

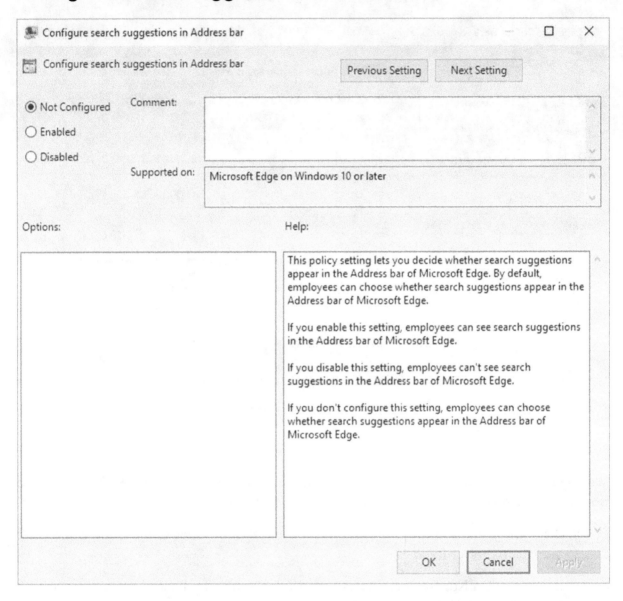

Microsoft Edge displays search suggestions as you type in the browser's address bar. The information that you enter is sent to Bing if the feature is enabled.

Microsoft Edge Settings:

- Open Microsoft Edge.
- Select Menu (the three dots), and Settings from the menu.
- Scroll down and click on "view advanced settings".
- Toggle "Show search and site suggestions as I type" to off.

Group Policy:

Computer Configuration > Administrative Templates > Windows Components > Microsoft Edge > Configure search suggestions in Address bar

- Enabled – Search suggestions are displayed when you type in the Microsoft Edge address bar
- Disabled – Search suggestion functionality is disabled.
- Not Configured – Users may enable or disable the feature in Microsoft Edge's settings.

Windows Registry:

Prevent Microsoft Edge from gathering Live Tile information

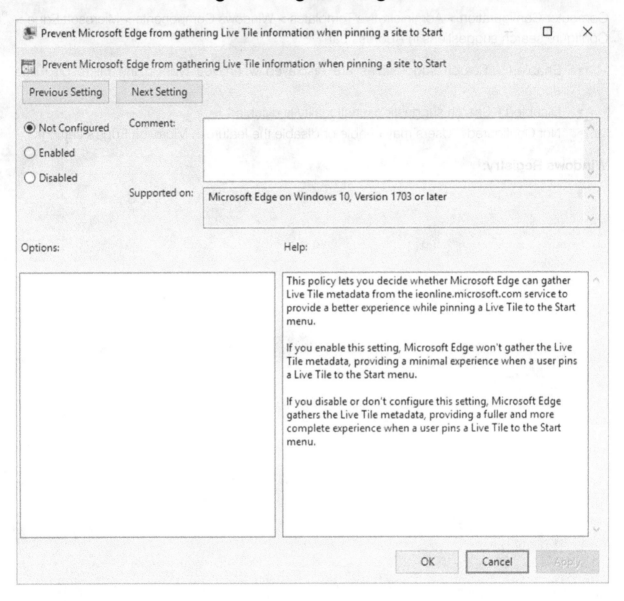

Microsoft Edge may contact ieonline.microsoft.com to gather Live Tile metadata to "provide a better experience" while pinning a Live Tile to the Start menu.

Group Policy:

Computer Configuration > Administrative Templates > Windows Components > Microsoft Edge > Prevent Microsoft Edge from gathering Live Tile information

- Enabled – If you enable the policy, Microsoft Edge won't contact ieonline.microsoft.com to gather Live Tile data.
- Disabled – Same as not configure. Microsoft will gather Live Tile metadata.

Prevent the First Run webpage from opening on Microsoft Edge

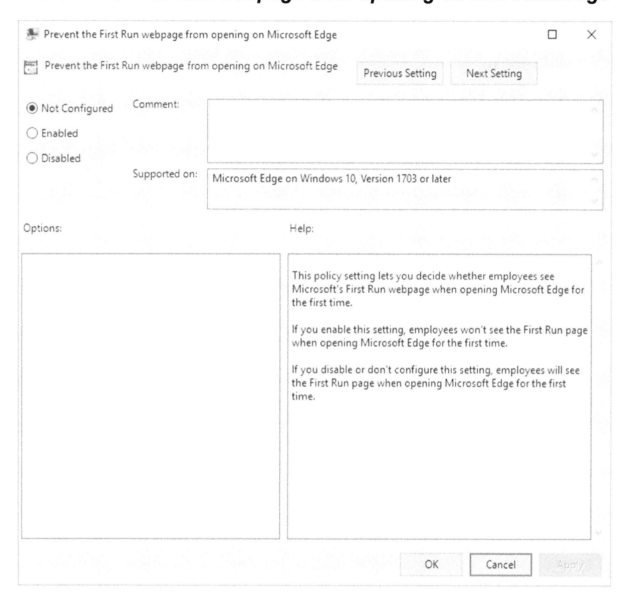

Microsoft Edge displays a First Run web page when a user starts the web browser for the first time. The browser's First Run page offers tips and highlights changes to improve a user's experience. This page is shown on first run after a new installation, but also when a new feature update is installed.

Group Policy:

Computer Configuration > Administrative Templates > Windows Components > Microsoft Edge > Prevent the First Run webpage from opening on Microsoft Edge

- Enabled –– The First Run page is not displayed when users open Microsoft Edge for the first time.
- Disabled – Same as not configured. The First Run page is shown.

Windows Registry:

Key: HKEY_LOCAL_MACHINE\Software\Policies\Microsoft\MicrosoftEdge\Main

Name: PreventFirstRunPage

Type: Dword

- 0 – The First Run page is shown in Microsoft Edge.
- 1 – The First Run page is blocked in Microsoft Edge.

Prevent using Localhost IP address for WebRTC

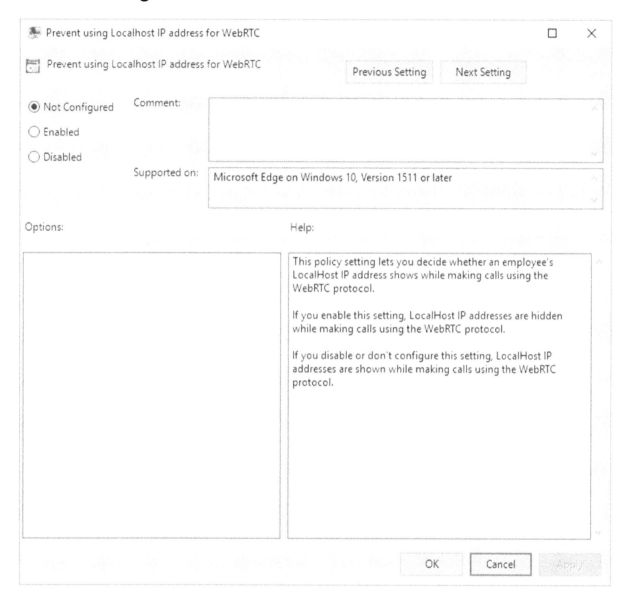

WebRTC may reveal the locahost IP address of a device that Microsoft Edge runs on when making calls using the WebRTC protocol.

Group Policy:

Computer Configuration > Administrative Templates > Windows Components > Microsoft Edge > Prevent using Localhost IP address for WebRTC

- Enabled – the Localhost IP address is not revealed when users are making calls using the WebRTC protocol.

- Disabled – Same as not configured. Localhost IP addresses are shown when making calls using the WebRTC protocol.

Windows Registry:

Key: HKEY_LOCAL_MACHINE\Software\Policies\Microsoft\MicrosoftEdge\Main

Name: HideLocalHostIP

Type: Dword

- 0 – Localhost IP addresses are shown when making WebRTC calls.
- 1 – Localhost IP addresses are not shown when making WebRTC calls.

OneDrive / File Synchronization

Prevent the usage of OneDrive for file storage

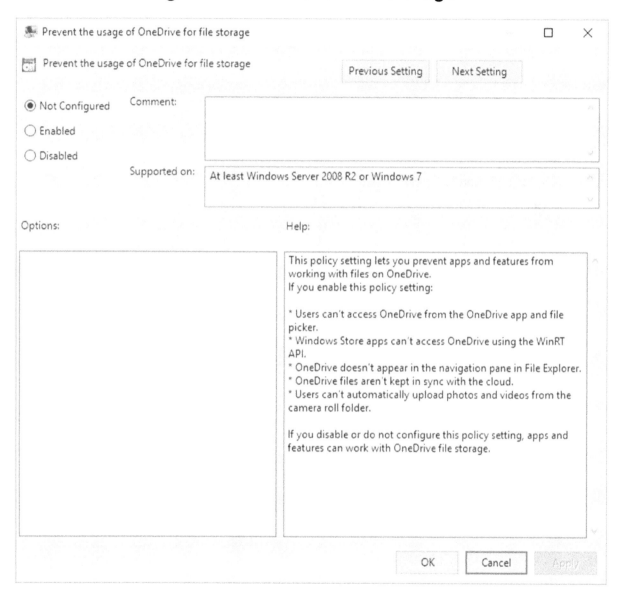

You may use this preference to disable OneDrive on the Windows 10 machine. Please note that this impacts several areas of the operating system:

- OneDrive files are not synchronized.
- The automatic uploading of photos and videos from the camera roll folder is disabled.
- OneDrive is not listed in File Explorer.

- OneDrive cannot be accessed from the OneDrive app or file picker.
- Windows Store apps cannot access OneDrive.

Group Policy: Computer Configuration > Administrative Templates > Windows Components > OneDrive > Prevent the usage of OneDrive for file storage

- Enable – This disables OneDrive on the Windows 10 device.
- Disable – Default, same as not configured. OneDrive is enabled.

Key: HKEY_LOCAL_MACHINE\SOFTWARE\Policies\Microsoft\Windows\OneDrive

Name: DisableFileSyncNGSC

Type: Dword

- A value of 0 means OneDrive is enabled.
- A value of 1 means Onedrive is disabled.

Do not Sync

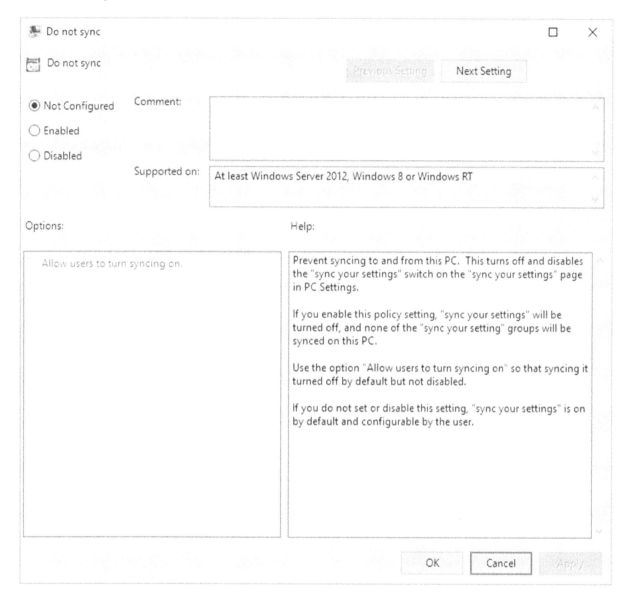

Control whether settings are synced on the device, and whether users may control the preference in the Settings application.

Windows 10 may synchronize the following settings or data:

- Theme
- Internet Explorer settings
- Passwords
- Language preferences

- Ease of accessed
- Other Windows settings

Group Policy

Computer Configuration > Administrative Templates > Windows Components > Sync your settings > Do not sync

- Enabled – Sync your settings is turned off on the device, and no data that is listed under "sync your settings" is synchronized. You may set "allow users to turn syncing on, to allow users to override the default.
- Disabled – Sync your setting is on by default, and users may control it.

Windows Registry

Key: HKEY_LOCAL_MACHINE\SOFTWARE\Policies\Microsoft\Windows\SettingSync

Name: DisableSettingSync

Type: Dword

- 1 – Sync your Settings is enabled.
- 2 – Sync your Settings is disabled.

Key: HKEY_LOCAL_MACHINE\SOFTWARE\Policies\Microsoft\Windows\SettingSync

Name: DisableSettingSyncUserOverride

Type: Dword

- 1 – Users may not override the default value of Sync your settings.

Do not Sync Application Settings

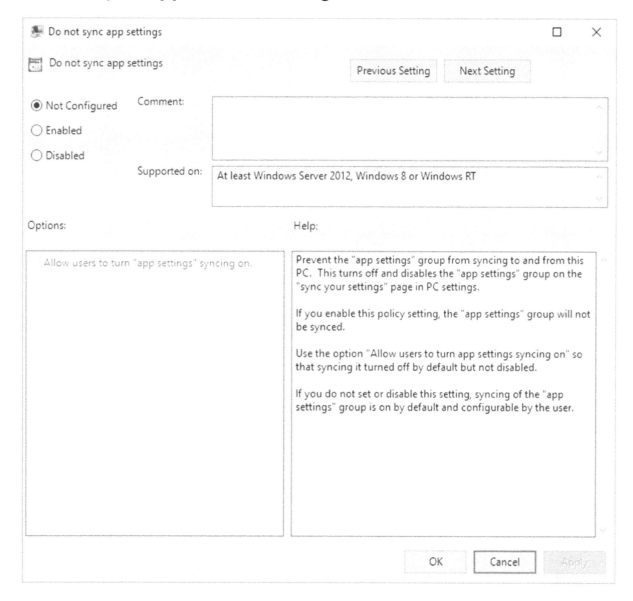

This policy may prevent the synchronization of application settings from one PC to another.

Group Policy: Computer Configuration > Administrative Templates > Windows Components > Sync your settings > Do not sync app settings

- Enabled – This prevents the synchronization of application settings. You may set the "allow users to turn app settings sync on" to give users an option to turn the functionality back on.
- Disabled – App syncing is on by default, and users may control the preference in the Settings application.

Key: HKEY_LOCAL_MACHINE\SOFTWARE\Policies\Microsoft\Windows\SettingSync

Value: DisableAppSyncSettingSync

Type: Dword

- 1 – The application sync setting is enabled.
- 2 – The synchronization of individual application settings is disabled.

Key: HKEY_LOCAL_MACHINE\SOFTWARE\Policies\Microsoft\Windows\SettingSync

Name: DisableAppSyncSettingSyncUserOverride

Type: Dword

- 1 – Users may not override the application sync setting

Do not sync passwords

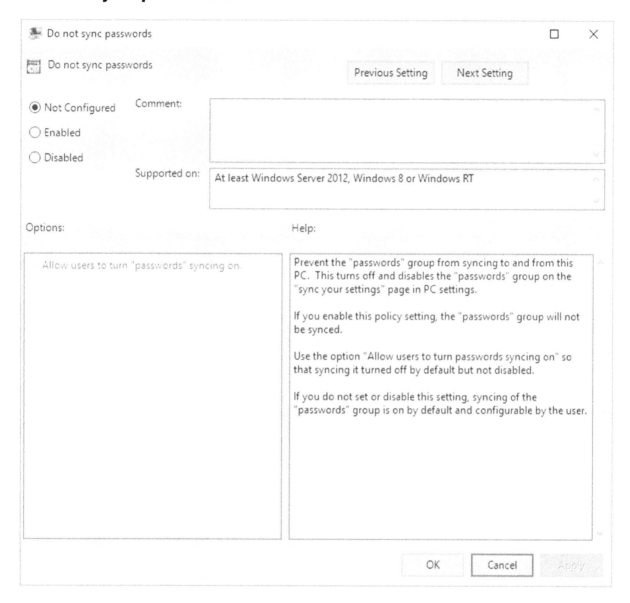

This setting controls whether passwords are synced as part of the "sync your settings" functionality of the Windows 10 operating system.

Group Policy: Computer Configuration > Administrative Templates > Windows Components > Sync your settings > Do not sync passwords

- Enabled – Passwords won't be synced by default if the policy is enabled. Administrators may check "allow users to turn passwords syncing on" to give users the option to turn the feature on in the Settings application.
- Disabled – Password syncing is enabled. Users may turn it off in the Settings application.

Key: HKEY_LOCAL_MACHINE\SOFTWARE\Policies\Microsoft\Windows\SettingSync

Name: DisableCredentialsSettingSync

Type: Dword

- 1 – Password syncing is enabled.
- 2 – Password syncing is disabled.

Key: HKEY_LOCAL_MACHINE\SOFTWARE\Policies\Microsoft\Windows\SettingSync

Name: DisableCredentialsSettingSyncUserOverride

Type: Dword

- 1 – Users may not enable password syncing in the Settings application.

Do not sync desktop personalization

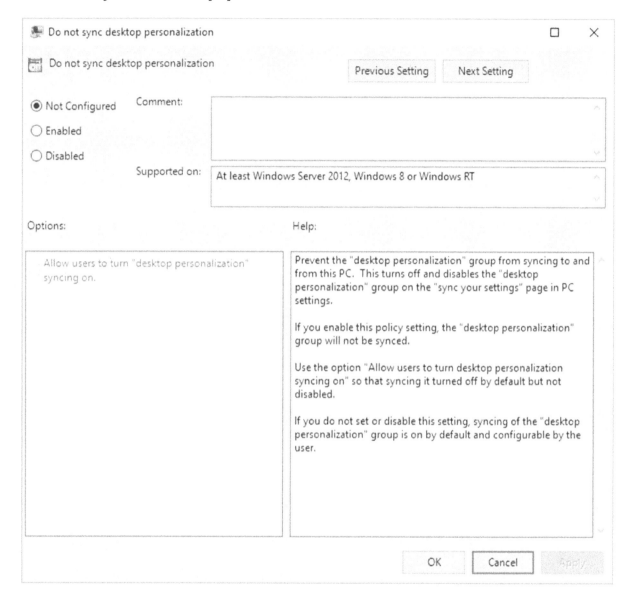

This policy determines whether a personalized desktop is synchronized or if the option is configurable in the Settings application.

Group Policy: Computer Configuration > Administrative Templates > Windows Components > Sync your settings > Do not sync desktop personalization

- Enabled – Desktop personalization syncing is turned off. Administrators may enable "allow users to turn desktop personalization syncing on", to give users control over the sync feature in the Settings application.

- Disabled – Desktop personalization is synced. Users may turn off the syncing in the Settings application.

Key: HKEY_LOCAL_MACHINE\SOFTWARE\Policies\Microsoft\Windows\SettingSync

Name: DisableDesktopThemeSettingSync

Type: Dword

- 1 – Desktop personalziation syncing is enabled.
- 2 – Desktop personalization syncing is disabled.

Key: HKEY_LOCAL_MACHINE\SOFTWARE\Policies\Microsoft\Windows\SettingSync

Name: DisableDesktopThemeSettingSyncUserOverride

Type: Dword

- 1 – Users may not change the sync setting in the Windows 10 Settings application.

Do not sync personalize

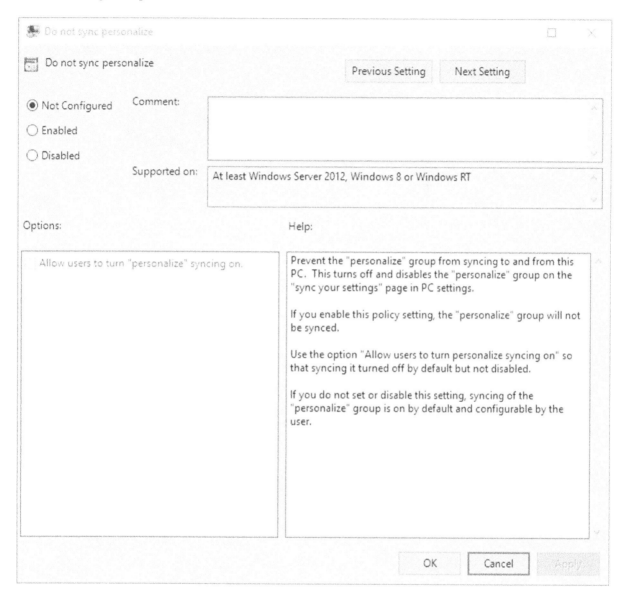

Windows 10 may sync personalized preferences, so that these become available on all Windows 10 devices the user signs in with a Microsoft account.

Group Policy: Computer Configuration > Administrative Templates > Windows Components > Sync your settings > Do not sync personalize

- Enabled – When the policy is enabled, "personalize" group data will not be synced. Administrators may enable "allow users to turn "personalize" syncing on, to provide users with options to turn the feature on manually.

- Disabled – Same as not configured. The "personalize" group is synced by default, and the user may disable the feature in the Settings interface.

Key: HKEY_LOCAL_MACHINE\SOFTWARE\Policies\Microsoft\Windows\SettingSync

Name: DisablePersonalizationSettingSync

Type: Dword

- 1 – The "personalize" group is synced.
- 2 – The "personalize" group is not synced.

Key: HKEY_LOCAL_MACHINE\SOFTWARE\Policies\Microsoft\Windows\SettingSync

Name: DisablePersonalizationSettingSyncUserOverride

Type: Dword

- 1 – Users may not change the personalize sync setting in the Windows 10 Settings application.

Do not sync start settings

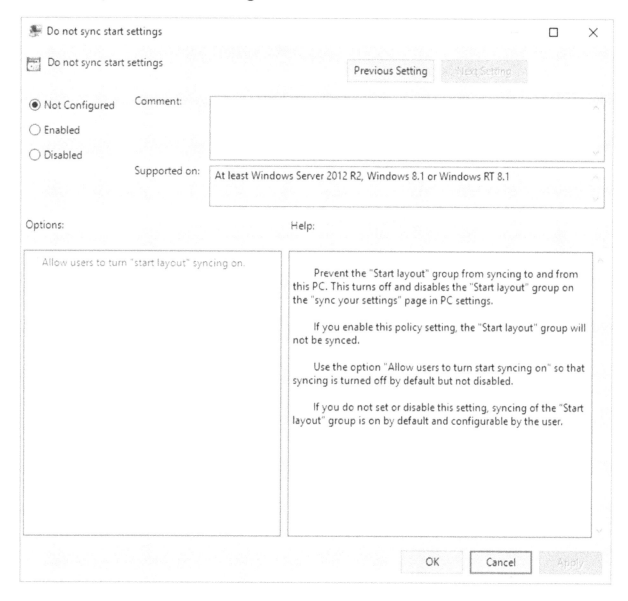

Windows 10 may sync the start layout so that it is available on all Windows 10 machines a user signs in using a Microsoft account.

Group Policy: Computer Configuration > Administrative Templates > Windows Components > Sync your settings > Do not sync start settings

- Enabled – The "start layout" group is not synced. Administrators may enable the "allow users to turn "start layout" syncing on, to provide users with options to enable the sync feature.

- Disabled – Same as not configured. "Start layout" syncing is enabled by default. Users may disable the syncing in the Settings UI.

Key: HKEY_LOCAL_MACHINE\SOFTWARE\Policies\Microsoft\Windows\SettingSync

Name: DisableStartLayoutSettingSync

Type: Dword

- 1 – The "start layout" group is synced.
- 2 – The layout of Start is not synced.

Key: DisableStartLayoutSettingSync

Name: DisableStartLayoutSettingSyncUserOverride

Type: Dword

- 1 – Users are not allowed to select whether they want the "start layout" to sync or not.

Do not sync browser settings

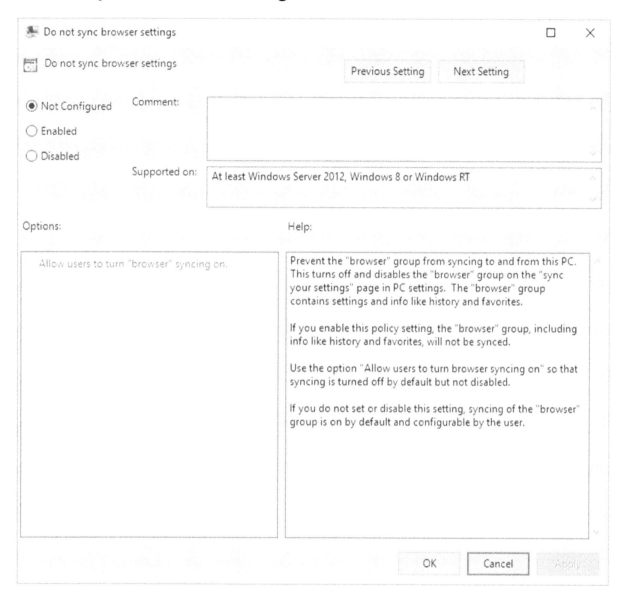

This policy may be used to prevent browser settings such as the browsing history or favorites from being synced.

Group Policy: Computer Configuration > Administrative Templates > Windows Components > Sync your settings > Do not sync browser settings

- Enabled – The "browser" group and its data won't be synced. Administrators may enable "Allow users to turn "browser" syncing on, to provide users with an option to enable the sync option in the Settings application.

- Disabled – Same as not configured. Browser data is synced by default. Users may disable the syncing in the Settings application.

Key: HKEY_LOCAL_MACHINE\SOFTWARE\Policies\Microsoft\Windows\SettingSync

Name: DisableWebBrowserSettingSync

Type: DWORD

- 1 – Web browser syncing is enabled.
- 2 – Web browser syncing is disabled.

Key: HKEY_LOCAL_MACHINE\SOFTWARE\Policies\Microsoft\Windows\SettingSync

Name: DisableWebBrowserSettingSyncUserOverride

Type: DWORD

- 1 – Users are not allowed to override the web browser sync setting.

Do not sync other Windows settings

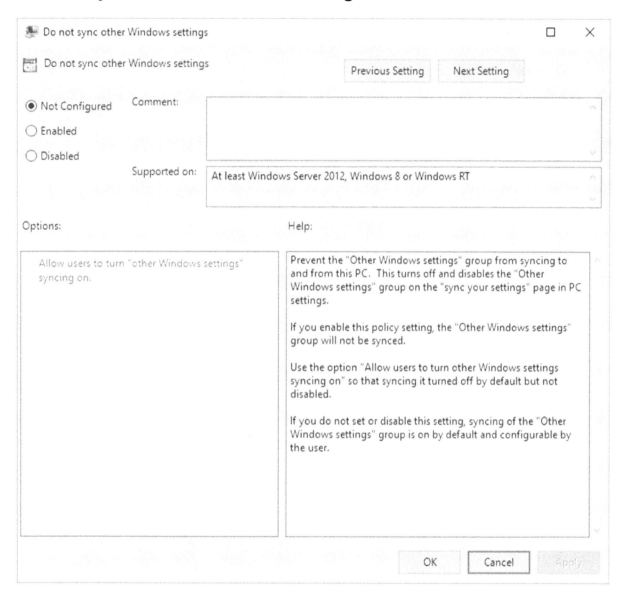

This policy may be used to prevent that other Windows settings are synced. It is unclear what "other Windows settings" includes when it comes to synchronization.

Group Policy: Computer Configuration > Administrative Templates > Windows Components > Sync your settings > Do not sync other Windows settings.

- Enabled – The synchronization of "other Windows settings" is disabled. Administrators may check "Allow users to turn other Windows settings syncing on" to give users an option to enable the syncing in the Settings application.

- Disabled – Same as not configured. Windows 10 will sync "other Windows settings" by default. Users may turn off the feature in the Settings UI.

Key: HKEY_LOCAL_MACHINE\SOFTWARE\Policies\Microsoft\Windows\SettingSync

Name: DisableWindowsSettingSync

Type: DWORD

- 1 – The default value. "Other Windows settings" are synced.
- 2 – The syncing of "Other Windows settings" is disabled.

Key: HKEY_LOCAL_MACHINE\SOFTWARE\Policies\Microsoft\Windows\SettingSync

Name: DisableWindowsSettingSyncUserOverride

Type: DWORD

- 1 – Users may not override the "Other Windows syncing" setting in the Settings UI.

Do not sync on metered connections

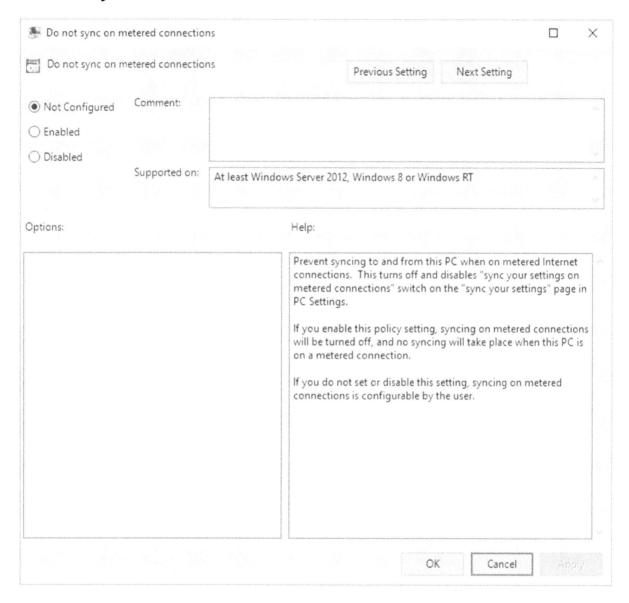

This policy defines whether synchronization of data is enabled when the PC is on a metered Internet connection.

Group Policy: Computer Configuration > Administrative Templates > Windows Components > Sync your settings > Do not sync on metered connections

- Enabled – Syncing is turned off when the PC is connected using a metered connection.
- Disabled – Same as not configured. Syncing on metered connections is enabled by default, but can be turned off by the user.

Key: HKEY_LOCAL_MACHINE\SOFTWARE\Policies\Microsoft\Windows\SettingSync

Name: DisableSyncOnPaidNetwork

Type: Dword

- 1 – Syncing is disabled when the PC is on a metered Internet connection.

SmartScreen

Configure Windows Defender SmartScreen (Edge)

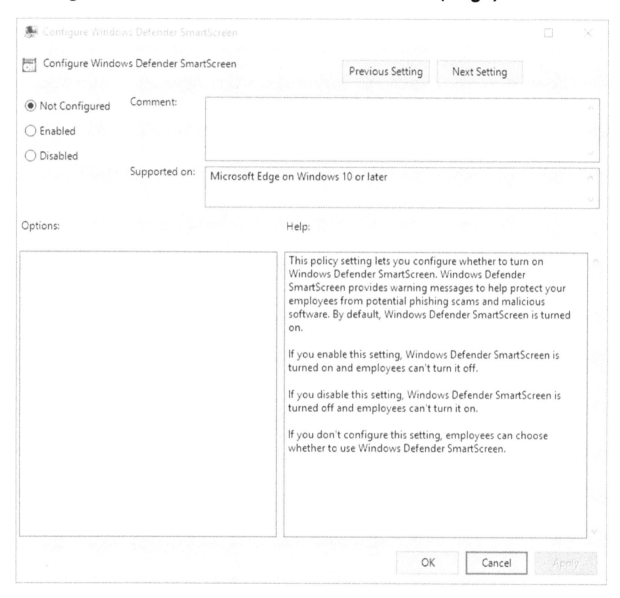

This policy defines whether Windows Defender SmartScreen is enabled when Microsoft Edge is used as the system browser. SmartScreen provides defense against malware, phishing and other threats that originate on the Internet.

Group Policy

Computer Configuration > Administrative Templates > Windows Components > Microsoft Edge > Configure Windows Defender SmartScreen Filter

Windows Server Group Policy: Computer Configuration > Administrative Templates > Windows Components > Microsoft Edge > Configure SmartScreen Filter

- Enabled – Windows Defender SmartScreen is turned on, and users cannot turn it off.
- Disabled – Windows Defender SmartScreen is turned off, and users cannot turn it on.
- Not Configured – Employees may enable or disable Windows Defender SmartScreen.

Windows Registry

Key: HKEY_CURRENT_USER\SOFTWARE\Microsoft\Windows\CurrentVersion\AppHost.

Name: EnableWebContentEvaluation

Type: Dword

- 0 – Windows Defender SmartScreen is disabled.
- 1 – Windows Defender SmartScreen is enabled.

Key: HKEY_LOCAL_MACHINE\Software\Policies\Microsoft\Windows\System

Name: EnableSmartScreen

Type: Dword

- 0 – Windows Defender SmartScreen is disabled.
- 1 – Windows Defender SmartScreen is enabled.

Configure Windows Defender SmartScreen

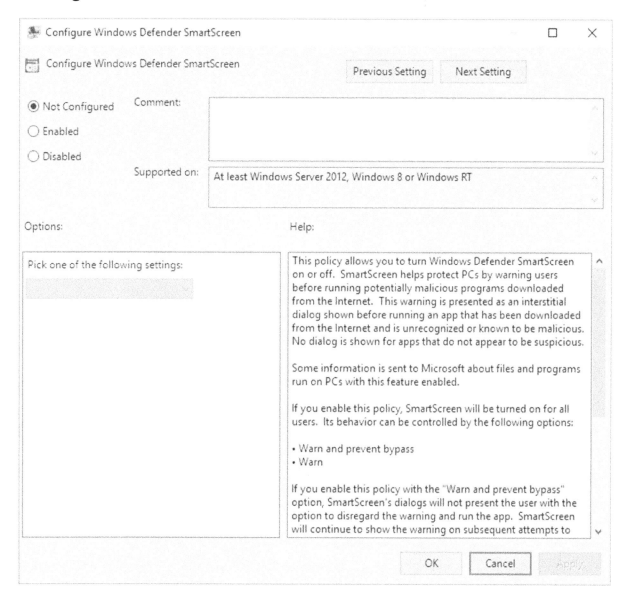

This policy defines whether Windows Defender SmartScreen is enabled on the Windows PC. The feature protects the PC against programs downloaded from the Internet that are not recognized by Windows Defender.

Information on the files and programs that are run on the PC are sent to Microsoft when the feature is enabled.

Group Policy

Computer Configuration > Administrative Templates > Windows Components > File Explorer > Configure Windows Defender SmartScreen

- Enabled – When you enable the policy, you may set it to "warn and prevent bypass", or "warn". The first pick provides users with the means to run the file by bypassing the warning, the second won't allow users to do that.
- Disabled – Windows Defender SmartScreen will be turned off.
- Not Configured – SmartScreen is enabled, but users may change the setting.

Windows Registry

Key: HKEY_LOCAL_MACHINE \SOFTWARE\Microsoft\Windows\CurrentVersion\Explorer

Name: SmartScreenEnabled

Type: String value

- Off – This disables SmartScreen Filter.
- RequireAdmin – Administrator approval required before an unrecognized Internet program is run.
- Prompt – Display a warning before running an unrecognized Internet program, but don't require Admin approval to run it.

Key: HKEY_LOCAL_MACHINE \SOFTWARE\WOW6432Node\Microsoft\Windows\CurrentVersion\ Explorer

Name: SmartScreenEnabled

Type: String value

- Off – This disables SmartScreen Filter.
- RequireAdmin – Administrator approval required before an unrecognized Internet program is run.
- Prompt – Display a warning before running an unrecognized Internet program, but don't require Admin approval to run it.

Windows Error Reporting

Windows Error Reporting allows Microsoft to gain information about Windows system, feature and application errors. It furthermore provides users and administrators with options to receive information about potential solutions for encountered issues.

Disable Windows Error Reporting

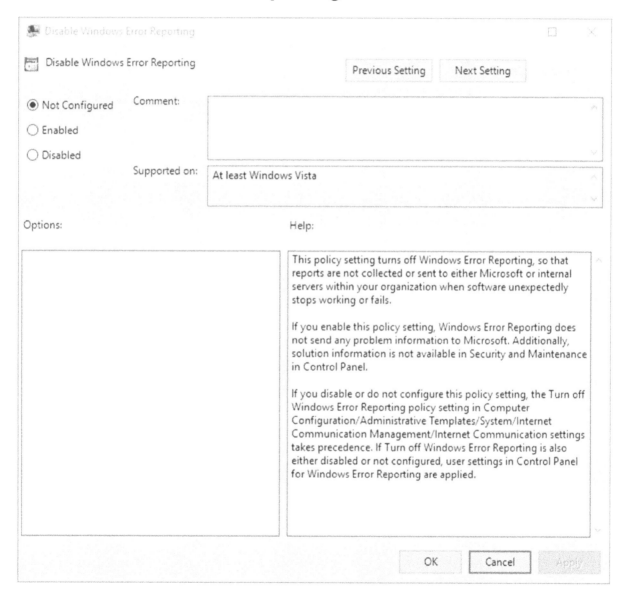

The policy turns the Windows Error Reporting feature off. This has the effect that reports are not collected or sent to Microsoft or internal servers when software fails or stops working.

Group Policy:

User Configuration > Administrative Templates > Windows Components > Windows Error Reporting > Disable Windows Error Reporting

- Enabled – If you enable this policy, Windows Error Reporting is disabled. Solution information under Security and Maintenance is not available anymore when you disable error reporting.
- Disabled – Same as not configured. Windows Error Reporting is enabled. Note that this may be overridden by "Turn off Windows Error Reporting" policy setting in Computer Configuration/Administrative Templates/System/Internet Communication Management/ Internet Communication

Windows Registry:

Key: HKEY_LOCAL_MACHINE\SOFTWARE\Policies\Microsoft\Windows\Windows Error Reporting

Name: Disabled

Type: Dword

- 0 – Windows Error Reporting is enabled.
- 1 – Windows Error Reporting is disabled.

Do not send additional data

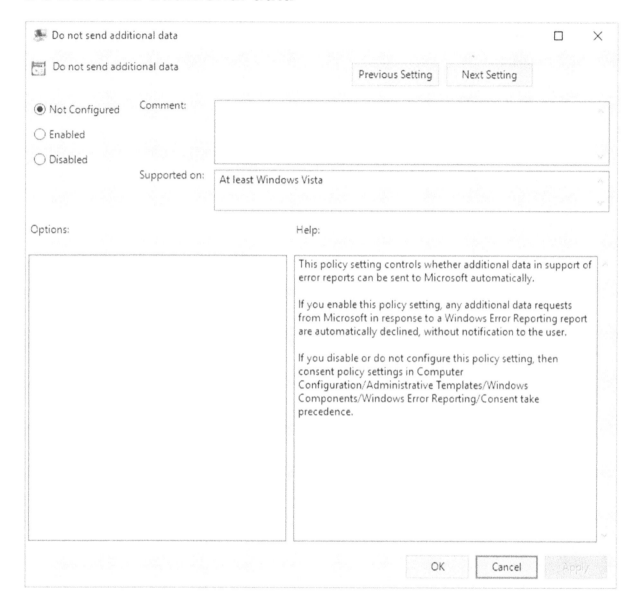

This defines whether additional data in "support of error reports" can be sent to Microsoft automatically.

Group Policy:

User Configuration > Administrative Templates > Windows Components > Windows Error Reporting > Disable Windows Error Reporting

- Enabled – Any additional data requests from Microsoft in response to Windows Error Reporting are declined automatically without user notification.

- Disabled – Same as not configured. The feature is enabled. Note that consent policy settings in Computer Configuration/Administrative Templates/Windows Components/Windows Error Reporting/Consent take precedence.

Windows Registry:

Key: HKEY_LOCAL_MACHINE\SOFTWARE\Policies\Microsoft\Windows\Windows Error Reporting

Name: DontSendAdditionalData

Type: Dword

- 0 – Send additional data
- 1 – Do not send additional data.

Windows Media Player

Windows Media Player is a long-standing media player that ships with Windows 10. It plays audio and video files, and supports a variety of features such as Internet streaming or looking up information online for media that is played using it.

Prevent Music file Media Information Retrieval

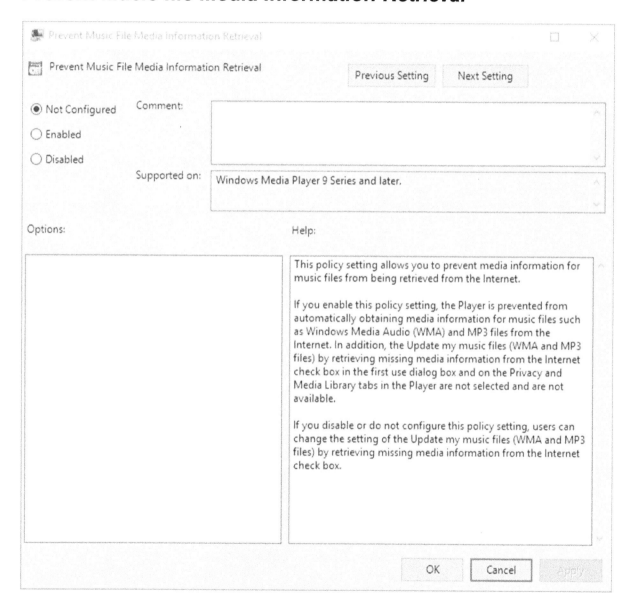

Windows Media Player may download media information from the Internet for music files that are played in the application to display the information in its interface.

Group Policy:

User Configuration > Administrative Templates > Windows Components > Windows Media Player > Prevent Music File Media Information Retrieval

- Enabled – Windows Media Player is prevented from retrieving media information for music files. Additionally, Update My Music files is not available in the player.
- Disabled – The default setting. Windows Media Player retrieves music information from the Internet, and users may use the update my music files option as well.

Windows Registry:

Key: HKEY_CURRENT_USER\SOFTWARE\Policies\Microsoft\WindowsMediaPlayer

Name: PreventMusicFileMetadataRetrieval

Type: Dword

- 0 – The default value. Windows Media Player may retrieve music information automatically from the Internet.
- 1 – A value of 1 disables the feature.

Prevent CD and DVD Media Information Retrieval

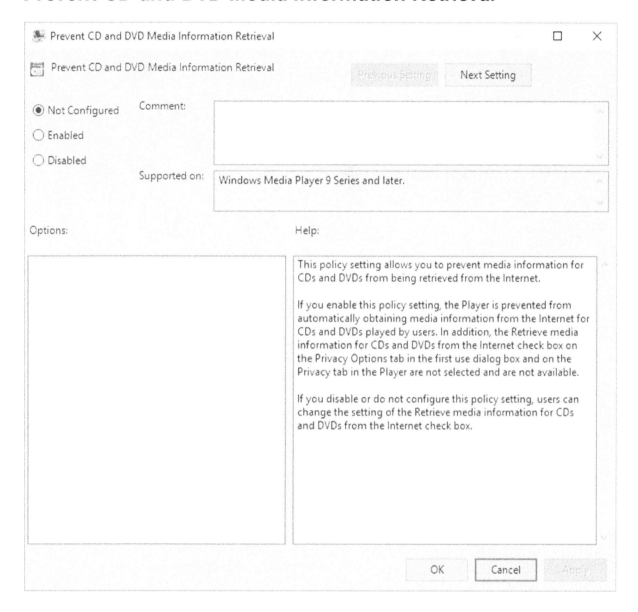

Windows Media Player may look up information on CDs or DVDs that are loaded while it is running by querying Internet servers. Information that it retrieves are then displayed in the media player.

Group Policy:

User Configuration > Administrative Templates > Windows Components > Windows Media Player > Prevent CD and DVD Media Information Retrieval

- Enabled – Windows Media Player is blocked from retrieving CD or DVD media information from the Internet. The Retrieve Media option is not available.

- Disabled – The default setting. Windows Media Player may retrieve media information for CDs or DVDs. The Retrieve Media checkbox is available.

Windows Registry:

Key: HKEY_CURRENT_USER\ Software\ Policies\ Microsoft\ WindowsMediaPlayer

Name: PreventCDDVDMetadataRetrieval

Type: Dword

- 0 – The default value. Windows Media Player may look up CD or DVD metadata.
- 1 – This prevents Windows Media Player from doing so.

Prevent Radio Station Preset Retrieval

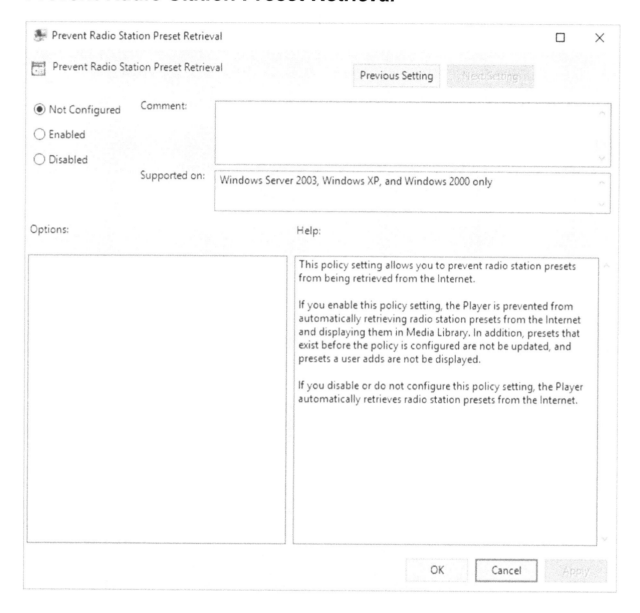

Windows Media Player may retrieve Radio Station presets from the Internet.

Group Policy:

User Configuration > Administrative Templates > Windows Components > Windows Media Player > Prevent Radio Station Preset Retrieval

- Enabled – Windows Media Player is blocked from retrieving Radio Station presets automatically from the Internet, and displaying them in the library. Presets that existed before the policy is set to enabled are not updated, and presets a user adds are not displayed.

- Disabled – The default setting. Windows Media Player retrieves and updates Radio Station presets.

Windows Registry:

Key: HKEY_CURRENT_USER\ Software\ Policies\ Microsoft\ WindowsMediaPlayer

Name: PreventRadioPresetsRetrieval

Type: Dword

- 0 – The default value. Windows Media Player may retrieve Radio Station presets.
- 1 – This prevents Windows Media Player from doing so.

Prevent Windows Media DRM Internet Access

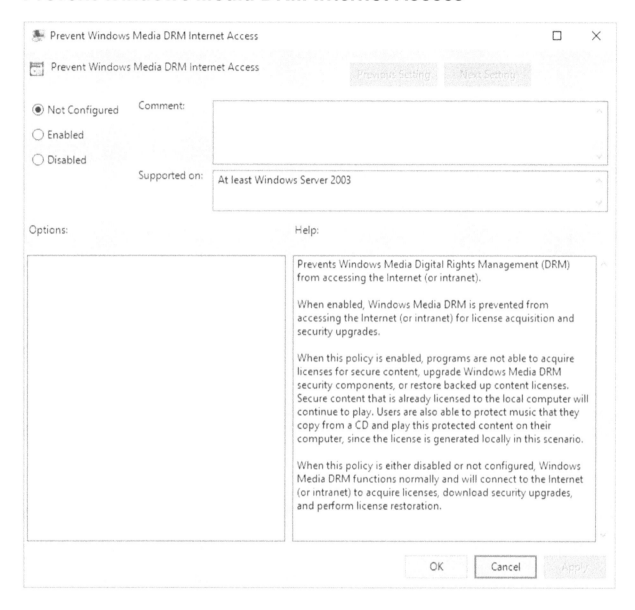

Windows Media Player may acquire licenses for secure content, upgrade Windows Media DRM security components, or restore backed up content licenses automatically.

Group Policy:

Computer Configuration > Administrative Templates > Windows Components > Windows Media Digital Rights Management > Prevent Windows Media DRM Internet Access

- Enabled – Windows Media Player is blocked from acquiring DRM licenses or performing other DRM related operations. This won't affect media with DRM that is already on the local computer and already licensed.
- Disabled – The default value. Windows Media Player may obtain digital licenses, and perform other DRM tasks.

Windows Registry:

Key: HKEY_LOCAL_MACHINE\ Software\ Policies\ Microsoft\ WMDRM

Name: DisableOnline

Type: Dword

- 0 – The default value. Media Player may connect to the Internet for DRM license retrievals and updates of DRM functionality.
- 1 – Windows Media Player is blocked and cannot retrieve digital licenses online anymore.

Windows Update

Windows Update is an essential component of the Windows 10 operating system. It is a built-in updating system that checks, downloads, and installs updates automatically or on user request depending on how it is configured.

The default configuration is set to automatic. This means that Windows Update will query Microsoft servers automatically in intervals for updates (the default is once per hour on Windows 10 Pro).

All updates receive a rating by Microsoft that is an indicator of their importance. Windows Update on Windows 10 is configured to download and install critical and important updates automatically by default.

Optional updates, and those that require user input, for instance by accepting terms, are not downloaded and installed automatically.

Windows Update is a good feature for the most part. It ensures that Windows devices receive the latest security patches and updates, so that they are protected against attacks that target known vulnerabilities.

Microsoft changed how updates are delivered on Windows 10 however. It introduced cumulative updates instead of individual updates for each patch that it releases.

This means that it is no longer possible to decide on a per-update basis if the update should be installed on a machine or not; it is all or nothing on Windows 10.

The only options that Windows 10 administrators and users have is to decide when they want to install updates.

Patches may reset privacy settings or introduce new privacy related features to Windows 10. Unlike on Windows 7 or Windows 8, Microsoft does not release a security-only update for Windows 10 on each Patch Tuesday.

This means that you end up with an all or nothing approach that is bad from a user's point of view.

Windows Update Suggestions

I recommend the following when it comes to Windows Update:

1. Always create a backup prior to installing Windows updates. This ensures that you can go back to a previous version of Windows if the installation goes wrong, if the update causes issues on the system, or if changes are made that you want reversed.
2. Check the changelogs for updates, and read sites that write about new updates that are released for Windows 10. This provides you with information on the updates, and also user

comments on sites that allow them so that you may know in advance if an update is broken for instance.

3. Security patches are important. Generally speaking, it is recommended to install those on the Windows 10 machine as soon as possible.

4. Verify that settings have not changed after an update has been installed on a Windows 10 machine.

Windows Update Download and Upload sources

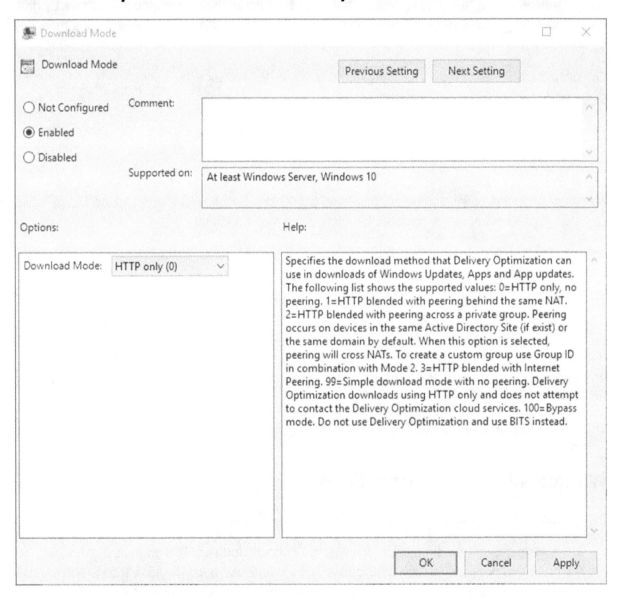

Windows 10 may use other sources than Microsoft servers to download updates to a local machine. These sources may be on the same LAN, a domain, or even on the Internet.

Bandwidth of the local system may be used therefore to distribute parts of Windows updates to third-party Internet users who run Windows 10 as well.

The best setting depends largely on the environment you use the computer in. If you use a single computer, you may not want to enable network or Internet updating. The reason why I recommend that is that it may save you quite a bit of bandwidth, and ensures that your PC's bandwidth is not used to transfer updates to third-party systems on the Internet that you don't know anything about.

If the device is in a local area network with other Windows 10 devices, it may make sense to enable direct and Lan peering, as bandwidth may be saved as a consequence.

Group Policy:

Computer Configuration > Administrative Templates > Windows Components > Delivery Optimization > Download Mode

- HTTP Only – No Peering.
- LAN – HTTP and peering behind the same NAT.
- Group – HTTP and peering on the same domain or in the same Active Directory Site (cross NAT)
- Internet – HTTP and Internet peering.
- Simple – No peering and does not try to contact the Delivery Optimization Service.
- Bypass – Do not use Delivery Optimization, and use BITS instead.

Windows Registry:

Key: HKEY_LOCAL_MACHINE\SOFTWARE\Policies\Microsoft\Windows\DeliveryOptimization

Name: DODownloadMode

Type: Dword

- 0 – Feature is disabled.
- 1 – Accept only peers on the same NAT.
- 2 – Accept local network / private peering (same domain).
- 3 – Internet Peering.
- 99 – Simple Download Mode.
- 100 – Bypass Mode.

Microsoft introduced a new feature in the Fall Creators Update for Windows 10 that gives users some control over the download and upload limits.

These have been available as Group Policy options in previous versions already, but they are listed in the Settings UI as well now.

Settings:

Settings application > Update & Security > Windows Update > Advanced Options > Delivery Optimization > Advanced Options.

Windows optimizes bandwidth dynamically by default. These options provide users with settings to limit the feature in the following ways:

- Limit download bandwidth.
- Limit upload bandwidth.
- Set monthly upload limit.

Group Policy:

Computer Configuration > Administrative Templates > Windows Components > Delivery Optimization

- Maximum Download Bandwidth (percentage)
- Maximum Download Bandwidth (KB/s)
- Max Upload bandwidth (in KB/s)
- Monthly Upload Data Cap (in GB)

Configure Automatic Updates

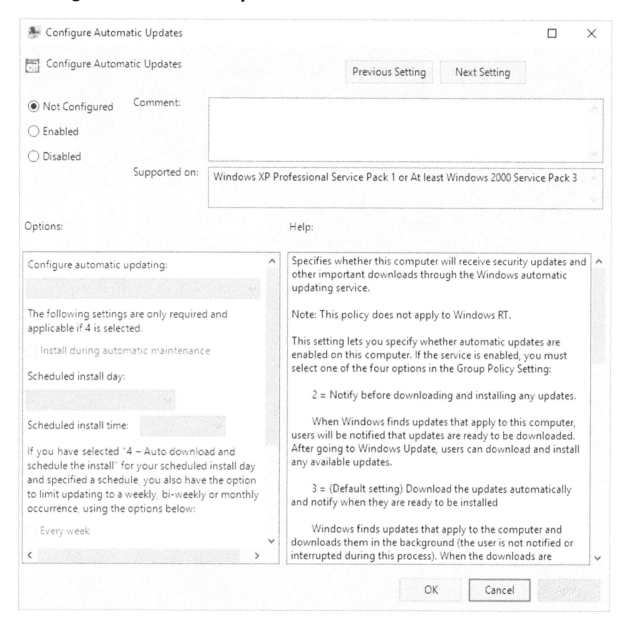

This policy provides you with options to change the default updating behavior of Windows Update. You can use it to configure automatic updating and scheduled updating.

Group Policy:

Computer Configuration > Administrative Templates > Windows Components > Windows Update > Configure Automatic Updates

- Enabled – When you enable the policy, you need to select one out of four options that define the PCs automatic updating behavior.

  ° Notify for download and auto install
  ° Auto download and notify for install (default)
  ° Auto download and schedule the install

    - Install during automatic maintenance
    - Scheduled install day and time
    - Install updates for other Microsoft products

  ° Allow local admin to choose setting.

- Disabled – If this policy is disabled, updates must be downloaded and installed manually using Windows Update.

Wi-Fi

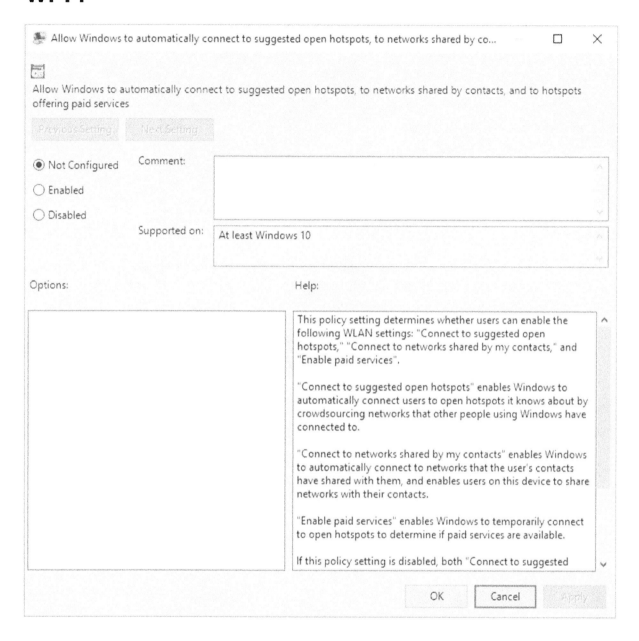

Microsoft Windows 10 supported a feature called Wi-Fi Sense up until recently. This feature was designed to improve the sharing of Wi-Fi passwords with others. Instead of having to hand out passwords directly to other users, Wi-Fi Sense could be used to share the passwords directly with the device.

The benefit was that the user who used the device did not know what the password was.

Microsoft removed the Wi-Fi Sense feature, and it is no longer available in its form. You do find other Wi-Fi related settings however that you may want to control.

The policy determines whether Wi-Fi features are enabled, and if users of the device may control the functionality.

Settings application:

Settings > Network & Internet > Wi-Fi

When you open the settings page, you get the following options which you may want to toggle to off if you don't plan on using them.

- Find paid plans for suggested open hotspots near me
- Connect to suggested open hotspots
- Hotspot 2.0 – Let me use Online Sign-Up to get connected

Group Policy:

Computer Configuration > Administrative Templates > Network > WLAN Service > WLAN Settings > Allow Windows to automatically connect to suggested open hotspots, to networks shared by contacts, and to hotspots offering paid services.

- Enabled – Same as not configured. Windows users may choose to enable or disable "connect to suggested open hotspots" and "connect to networks shared by my contacts" using the Settings application.
- Disabled – Wi-Fi Sense is turned off, and users cannot turn it back on.

Windows Registry

Key: HKEY_LOCAL_MACHINE\SOFTWARE\Microsoft\WcmSvc\wifinetworkmanager\config\

Name: AutoConnectAllowedOEM

Type: Dword

- 0 – A value of 0 disables Wi-Fi Sense.

Misc

Disable Application Telemetry

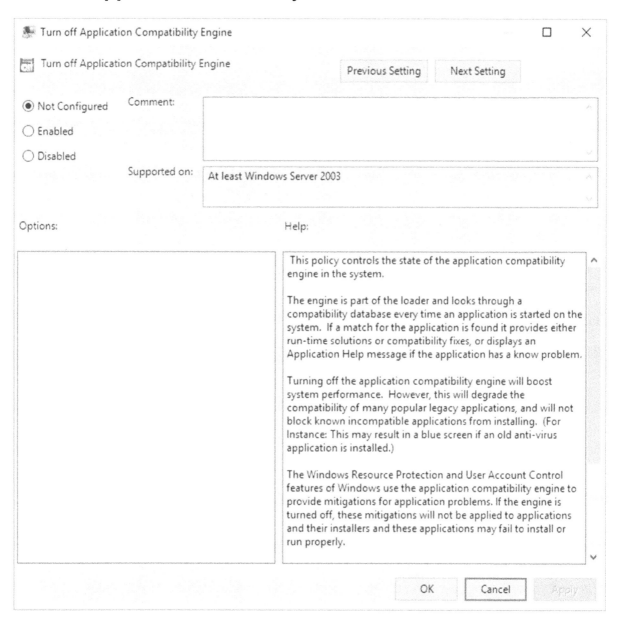

The Application Compatibility Engine checks whether an application that is run on the system is found in the compatibility database. If that is the case, it offers solutions and compatibility fixes, or an Application Help message if the problem is known.

Note: Windows Resource Protection and User Account Control rely on the Application Compatibility Engine to provide solutions for known compatibility issues. If you turn off the feature, these mitigations are not applied, and installation or the start of programs with known compatibility issues may fail.

Systems may cache the value of this setting for performance purposes. You may need to restart the system before the change takes effect.

Microsoft notes that disabling the engine is useful in high load environments, for instance in server environments where applications may be loaded several hundred times per second.

Policy: Computer Configuration >Administrative Templates > Windows Components > Application Compatibility > Turn off Application Compatibility Engine

- Enabled: When you turn off the Application Compatibility Engine, you will improve system performance. It may however result in issues such as degrading the compatibility of legacy applications. It may also block incompatible programs from installing at all, or may result in crashes or blue screens.
- Disabled: Same as not configured. The Application Compatibility Engine runs.

Key: HKEY_LOCAL_MACHINE\SOFTWARE\Policies\Microsoft\Windows\AppCompat

Name: AITEnable

Value:

- 0 – Disables the Application Compatibility Engine.
- 1 – Same as if the Dword does not exist. Application Compatibility Engine is enabled.

Disable Inventory Collector

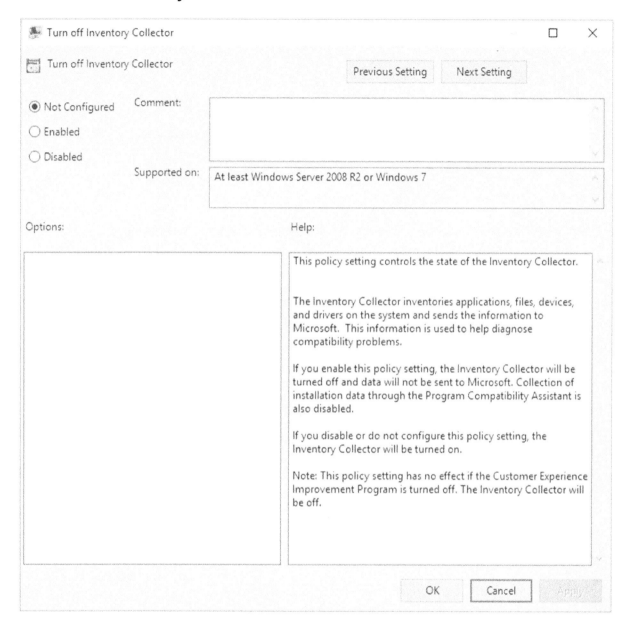

The Inventory Collector collects application, file, device, and driver inventory data on a system running Windows 10, and sends the information to Microsoft.

Microsoft states in the policy description that it uses the information to assist in the diagnosis of compatibility problems.

Note: The policy has no effect if the Customer Experience Improvement Program is disabled. The Inventory Collector is disabled then as well automatically.

Policy: Computer Configuration >Administrative Templates > Windows Components > Application Compatibility > Turn off Inventory Collector

- Enabled: If you enable the policy, the Inventory Collector is turned off, and data is no longer sent to Microsoft. This disables the collection of installation data through the Program Compatibility Assistant as well.
- Disabled: Same as not configured. Inventory Collector works normally.

Key: HKEY_LOCAL_MACHINE\SOFTWARE\Policies\Microsoft\Windows\AppCompat

Name: DisableInventory

Values:

- 0 – Same as if the Dword does not exit. Inventory Collector works normally.
- 1 – Disable the Inventory Collector.

Turn off downloading of game information

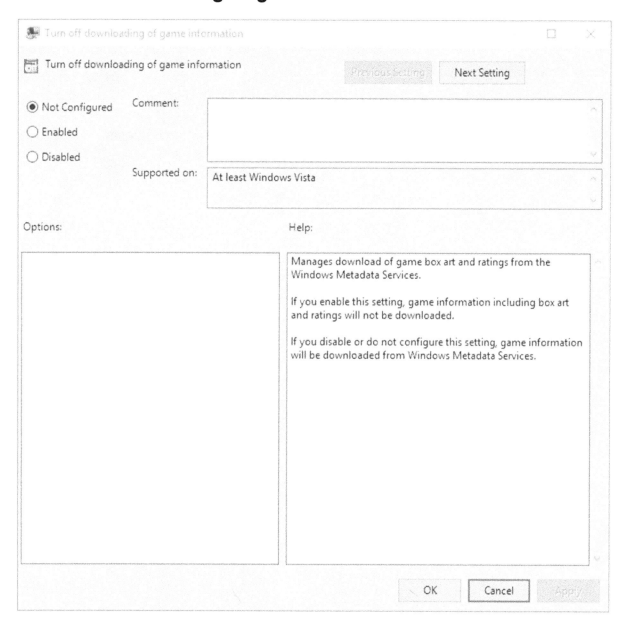

Windows may look up information about games online to retrieve game box art and ratings using Windows Metadata Services. This is part of the operating system's Game Explorer feature.

Policy: Computer Configuration > Administrative Templates > Windows Components > Game Explorer > Turn off downloading of game information

- Enabled – This blocks the downloading of game box art and ratings by querying Windows Metadata Services.

- Disabled – Same as not configured. Windows Metadata Services are used to download game box art and ratings.

Key: HKEY_LOCAL_MACHINE\SOFTWARE\Policies\Microsoft\Windows\GameUX

Name: DownloadGameInfo

Type: Dword

- 0 – The feature is turned off, Game Box Art and ratings are not downloaded.
- 1 – The feature is enabled.

Turn off automatic download and update of Map database

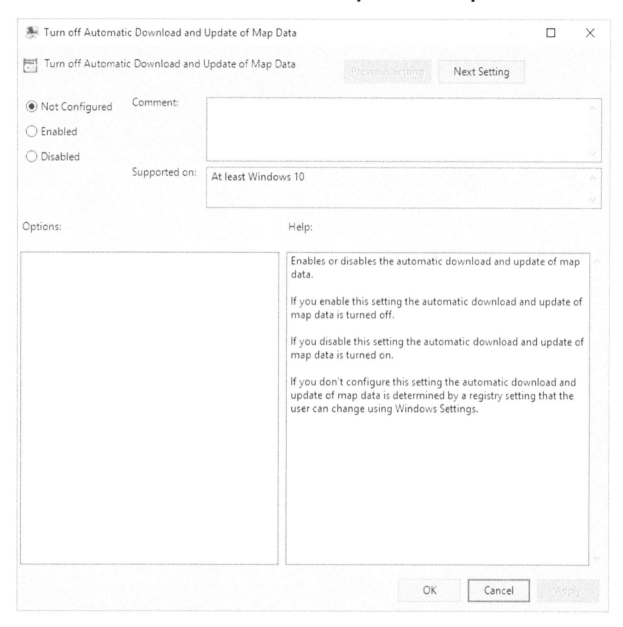

Windows 10 may download and update the map database automatically. The feature is controlled by these settings.

Policy: Computer Configuration > Administrative Templates > Windows Components > Maps > Turn off automatic download and update of Map database

- Enabled – When the setting is enabled, the automatic downloading and updating of map data is disabled.
- Disabled – Same as not configured. This means Map data is automatically download and updated.

Windows Services

Services are a core part of the Windows operating system. Changing their state, or disabling services altogether may result in functionality or stability issues on the system.

Generally speaking, it is suggested to leave the majority of services alone with the exception of Connected User Experiences and Telemetry, and Dmwappushservice. This chapter looks at some services that have privacy implications and explains what they do when they run.

Connected User Experiences and Telemetry

This is the main Telemetry service on Windows 10 machines. It manages the "event driven collection and transmission of diagnostic and usage information".

Dmwappushservice

The WAP Push Message Routing Service. Used to transfer data to Microsoft servers. Not a lot of information on this service.

Connected Devices Platform Service

CDPUserSvc_xxxxx

This service is used for Connected Devices Platform scenarios. Not a lot of information on this service either. May not want to disable if you use Bluetooth or wireless on the desktop. You may disable the service to see what happens though. If you run into connectivity issues with devices, you need to enable it again.

WINDOWS TASKS

Windows 10 ships with a number of scheduled tasks that are run regularly. Some of these tasks are used to collect Telemetry data, and transfer the data to Microsoft.

The following list focuses on tasks that collect Telemetry data.

Task Scheduler > Task Scheduler Library > Windows > Application Experience > Microsoft Compatibility Appraiser

> Collects program telemetry information if opted-in to the Microsoft Customer Experience Improvement Program.

Task Scheduler > Task Scheduler Library > Windows > Application Experience > Program Data Updater

Task Scheduler > Task Scheduler Library > Windows > Autochk > Proxy

> This task collects and uploads autochk SQM data if opted-in to the Microsoft Customer Experience Improvement program.

Task Scheduler > Task Scheduler Library > Windows > Customer Experience Improvement Program > Consolidator

> If the user has consented to participate in the Windows Customer Experience Improvement Program, this job collects and sends usage data to Microsoft

Task Scheduler > Task Scheduler Library > Windows > Customer Experience Improvement Program > KernelCeipTask

> The Kernel Ceip (Customer Experience Improvement Program) task collects additional information about the system and sends this data to Microsoft. If the user has not consented to participate in Windows CEIP, this task does nothing.

Task Scheduler > Task Scheduler Library > Windows > Customer Experience Improvement Program > USBCeip

> The USB CEIP (Customer Experience Improvement Program) task collects Universal Serial Bus related statistics and information about your machine and sends it ot the Windows Device Connectivity engineering group at Microsoft.

> The information received is used to help improve the reliability, stability, and overall functionality of USB in Windows. If the user has not consented to participate in Windows CEIP, this task does nothing.

Task Scheduler > Task Scheduler Library > Windows > DiskDiagnostic > Microsoft-Windows-DiskDiagnosticDataCollector

> The Windows Disk Diagnostic task reports general disk and system information to Microsoft for users participating in the Customer Experience Program.

Task Scheduler > Task Scheduler Library > Windows > DiskFootprint > Diagnostics

> Disk Footprint collects drive usage statistics, and submits them to Microsoft if the user consented to participate in Windows CEIP.

Task Scheduler > Task Scheduler Library > Microsoft > Office > OfficeTelemetryAgentFallBack2016

> This task initiates the background task for Office Telemetry Agent, which scans and uploads usage and error information for Office solutions.

Task Scheduler > Task Scheduler Library > Microsoft > Office > OfficeTelemetryAgentLogOn2016

> This task initiates the background task for Office Telemetry Agent, which scans and uploads usage and error information for Office solutions when a user logs on to the computer.

OFFICE TELEMETRY

Office Telemetry is a compatibility monitoring framework that Microsoft introduced in Office 2013 and Office 365 ProPlus that replaced the Office Migration Planning Manager, Office Code Compatibility Inspector, and Office Environment Assessment Tool of Office 2010.

Microsoft describes how Office Telemetry works in Office 2013 in the following way:

> Office Telemetry in Office 2013 works as follows: When an Office document or solution is loaded, used, closed, or raises an error in certain Office 2013 applications, the application adds a record about the event to a local data store. Each record includes a description of the problem and a link to more information. Inventory and usage data is also tracked.

Microsoft distinguishes between Office Telemetry tools and components. The Telemetry Dashboard and the Telemetry Log are tools, while Telemetry logging, the Telemetry agent, or Group Policy settings are considered Telemetry components.

Turn on Telemetry data collection

This setting allows you to enable or disable the data collection in Office used by the Telemetry Dashboard and the Telemetry log.

Note: You need to add the Office Administrative Template Files to the Group Policy to make the change in the Group Policy Editor. You find links to the template files under "Telemetry and Privacy" in the resource section at the end of this book.

Group Policy:

User Configuration > Administrative Templates > Microsoft Office 2016 > Telemetry Dashboard > Turn on Telemetry data collection

- Enabled – Office Telemetry Agent and Office applications will collect telemetry data. This includes Office application usage, a list of recent Office documents including file names, solutions usage, compatibility issues, and critical errors.
- Disabled – Same as not configured. Office Telemetry Agent and Office applications do not generate or collect telemetry data.

Windows Registry:

Key: HKCU\SOFTWARE\Policies\Microsoft\Office\16.0\osm

Name: Enablelogging

Type: Dword

- 0 – Logging is disabled.
- 1 – Logging is enabled.

ANNOYANCES

Remove Ads / Suggestions

Turn off all Windows Spotlight features

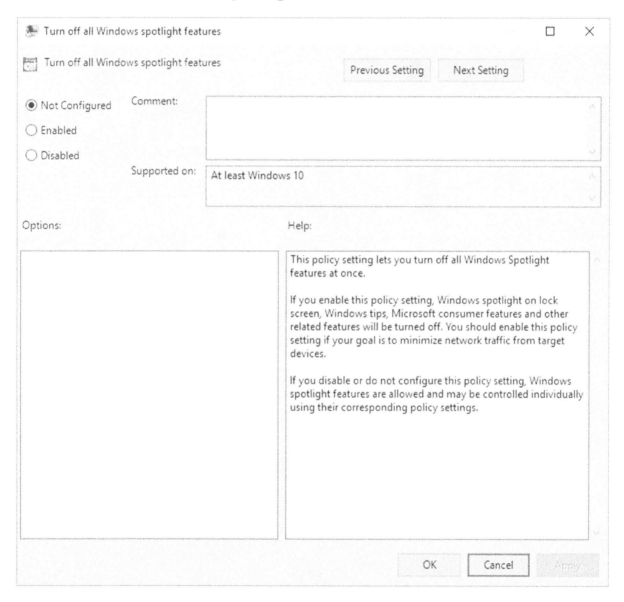

Windows Spotlight is a new feature of Windows 10. When enabled, it will download photos and images from Bing to display them on the lock screen of the Windows 10 device.

Windows Spotlight may display advertisement on the lockscreen, and also other content such as suggestions or tips.

This particular option disables Windows Spotlight completely.

Windows 10 Settings:

Open the Settings application and go to Personalization > Lock Screen. Locate the "Background" item on the page and use the menu to switch from Windows Spotlight to a different lock screen background.

Group Policy: (Enterprise only)

User Configuration > Administrative Templates > Windows Components > Cloud Content > Turn off all Windows Spotlight features

- Enabled – Windows Spotlight and all related features such as Windows tips on the lock screen are turned off.
- Disabled – Same as not configured. Windows Spotlight is enabled.

Do not suggest third-party content in Windows Spotlight

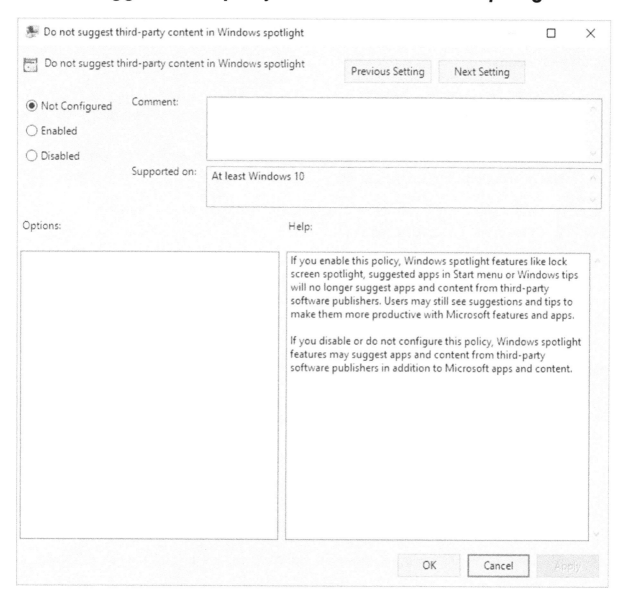

Windows Spotlight, a feature of Windows 10 that displays different wallpapers on the lock screen of the operating system, may suggest apps and content from third-party software publishers and Microsoft apps and content.

Group Policy

1. Open the Group Policy Editor.
2. Go to User Configuration > Administrative Templates > Windows Components > Cloud Content

3. Select Do not suggest third-party content in Windows spotlight.
   1. Set this policy to enabled, to disallow suggesting third-party content on the lock screen.
   2. Set this policy to disabled, to allow suggestions.

Windows Registry

1. Open the Windows Registry Editor.
2. Go to HKEY_CURRENT_USER\Software\Microsoft\Windows\CurrentVersion\ContentDelivery Manage
3. Right-click on ContentDeliveryManage, and select New > Dword (32-bit) Value.
4. Name it RotatingLockScreenEnabled.

   1. A value of 0 disables fun facts, tips, tricks and more on the lock screen.
   2. A value of 1 enables the feature.

5. Right-click on ContentDeliveryManage, and select New > Dword (32-bit) Value.
6. Name it RotatingLockScreenOverlayEnabled

   1. A value of 0 means disable.
   2. A value of 1 means enable.

Related Enterprise policies

- User Configuration > Administrative Templates > Windows Components > Cloud Content > Configure Windows Spotlight on Lock Screen

  ° If you set this to disabled, Windows Spotlight is turned off and users won't be able to select it as the lockscreen background.

- User Configuration > Administrative Templates > Windows Components > Cloud Content > Turn off the Windows Spotlight on Action Center

  ° If you enable this policy, Windows Spotlight notifications are no longer shown on Action Center.

- User Configuration > Administrative Templates > Windows Components > Cloud Content > Turn off the Windows Welcome Experience

  ° If you enable the policy, The Windows Welcome Experience will no longer display when there are updates and changes to Windows and its apps.

Show occasional suggestions in the Start Menu

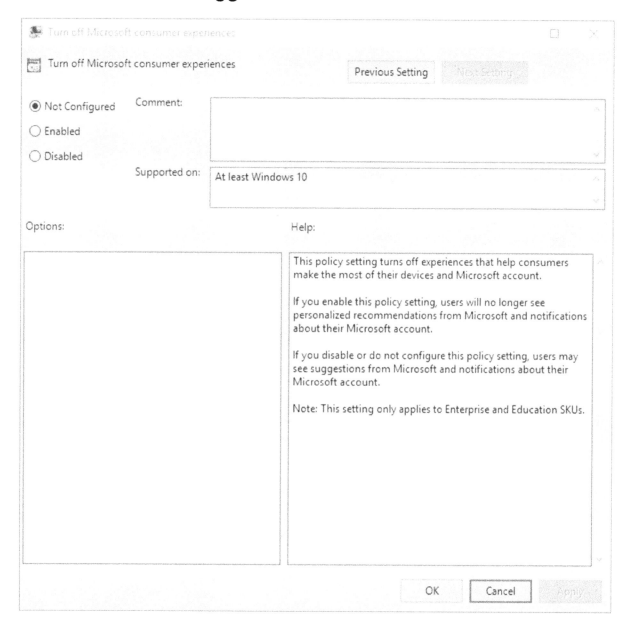

Windows 10 may display suggestions in the Start Menu, usually for applications that are installed (Edge) or not installed.

Group Policy

This policy setting turns off experiences that help consumers make the most of their devices and Microsoft account.

Note: Only applies to Enterprise and Education SKUs. Use the Registry method below instead if you run Home or Pro.

1. Open the Group Policy Editor.
2. Go to Computer Configuration > Administrative Templates > Windows Components > Cloud Content.
3. Select Turn off Microsoft Consumer Experience.

   1. Set the policy to enabled to turn off personalized recommendations from Microsoft, and notifications about the Microsoft Account.
   2. Set the policy to disabled, to allow recommendations and notifications.

Windows Registry

1. Open the Windows Registry Editor.
2. Go to HKEY_CURRENT_USER\Software\Microsoft\Windows\CurrentVersion\ContentDelivery Manager
3. Right-click on ContentDeliveryManager, and select New > Dword (32-bit) Value.
4. Name it SystemPaneSuggestionsEnabled.
   1. Set its value to 0 to disable suggestions in the Start Menu.
   2. Set its value to 1 to enable suggestions.

Windows Tips and Feedback

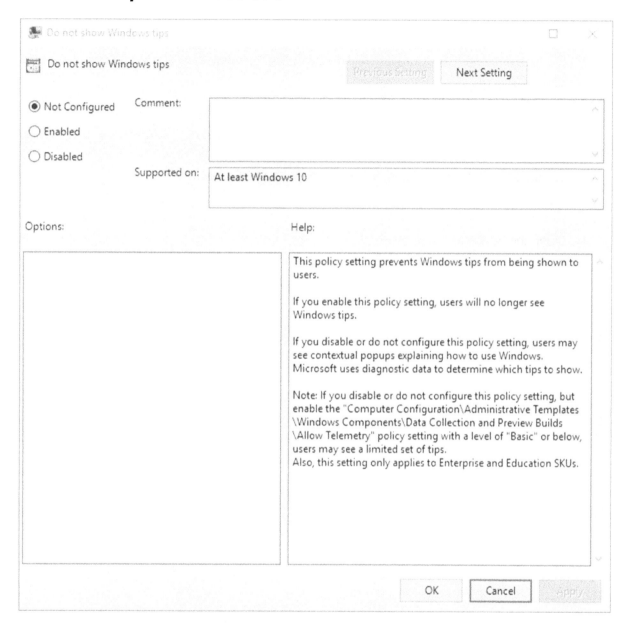

Windows 10 may display contextual popups that explain how to use Windows if the feature is enabled on the device. Microsoft uses diagnostic and usage data to determine which tips or suggestions to show to users.

Group Policy

This policy setting prevents Windows tips from being shown to users.

Note: Only applies to Enterprise and Education SKUs. Use the Registry method below instead if you run Home or Pro.

1. Open the Group Policy Editor.
2. Go to Computer Configuration > Administrative Templates > Windows Components > Cloud Content.
3. Select Do not show Windows tips.

   1. Set this policy to enabled, to disable contextual popups on the Windows desktop that show tips.
   2. Set this policy to disabled, to allow for tips to be displayed.

Windows Registry

1. Open the Windows Registry Editor.
2. Go to HKEY_CURRENT_USER\Software\Microsoft\CurrentVersion\ContentDeliveryManager
3. Right-click on ContentDeliveryManager, and select New > Dword (32-bit) Value.
4. Name it SoftLandingEnabled

   1. Set its value to 0 to disable the feature.
   2. Set its value to 1 to enable the feature.

Sync Provider Notifications in File Explorer

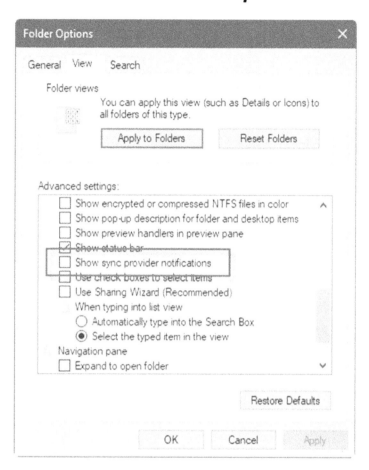

Windows 10 may display notifications in File Explorer, the default file browser of the Windows 10 operating system.

Folder Options

You may disable Sync Provider Notifications in the Folder Options window.

1. Open File Explorer.
2. Select View > Options.
3. Select View when the Folder Options window opens.
4. Locate "Show sync provider notifications" on the page, and remove the checkmark from the preference.
5. Click on Apply.
6. Click on OK.

Windows Registry

Key: HKEY_CURRENT_USER\SOFTWARE\Microsoft\Windows\CurrentVersion\Explorer\Advance

Name: ShowSyncProviderNotifications

Type: Dword

- 0 – The notifications are not shown in File Explorer.
- 1 – The notifications are enabled and shown in File Explorer.

Software

Software may assist you in managing Windows 10 operating systems. This book looks at privacy software for Windows 10, and other recommended software that may help you when you start to make privacy related changes to the operating system.

Windows 10 Privacy Software

The release of Windows 10 and the privacy controversy that surrounded it paved the way for more than a dozen software programs that were designed to improve privacy on Windows 10 machines in an easier environment.

The main advantage that these programs offer is that they bundle most of the privacy related tweaks so that you can adjust them according to your needs from a single interface.

You'd juggle between Group Policy entries, the Windows Settings application, the Windows Registry Editor, Services, Tasks and even the command line / PowerShell otherwise.

This chapter lists some of these tools, especially the ones that are updated regularly to reflect changes that Microsoft makes to Windows 10 with new feature releases.

Note: I recommend that you create a backup of the system before you run these tools. You can use a free backup software like Veeam Agent for Windows for that. Check out the "other recommended software" listing below for information on it.

Most programs below support the creation of System Restore points. While that is sufficient most of the time, it is better to be safe than sorry when it comes to this.

W10Privacy

Homepage: https://www.winprivacy.de/english-home/

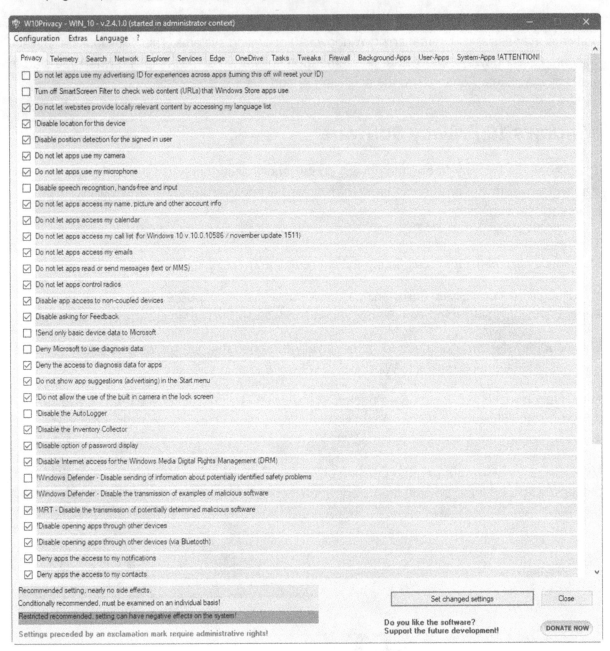

W10Privacy is a portable program that you can run from any location. It is recommended to run it with elevated rights – right-click and select run as administrator – as some functionality such as the creation of a System Restore point on start is not supported otherwise.

The application uses tabs to group the tweaks that it comes with and make orientation a bit easier. It color codes tweaks on top of that which helps distinguish between safe tweaks and tweaks that may or will impact functionality of the system.

You may use the program exclusively for making changes to privacy settings, for instance to block application access to features or disable web search.

The program checks all settings on Start and checks any that are already applied on the system. This helps you find settings that may require attention.

The Tweaks on their own are very powerful, but it does not end there.

The app supports the blocking of Microsoft servers in the hosts file to block connections, offers options to deal with tasks and services that are privacy related, and even provides you with options to uninstall applications.

ShutUp 10

Homepage: https://www.oo-software.com/en/shutup10

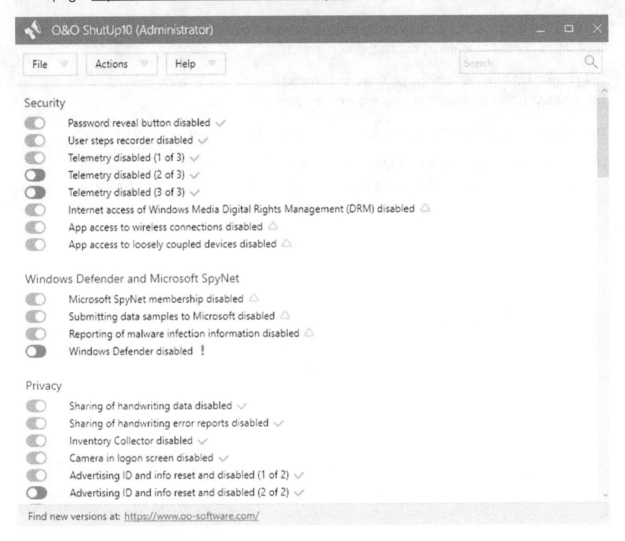

O&O ShutUp 10 is a portable program that you can run from any location. It lists all tweaks on a single page and not in tabs.

All tweaks are toggled using a slider that is displayed in front of them. A rating is displayed next to each tweak that indicates whether it is safe to make under any circumstances, something that could become problematic, or not recommended.

You may use the actions menu to apply all recommended tweaks at once, or go through the listing of tweaks manually to adjust them as you see fit.

ShutUp10 prompts you with a request to create a system restore point whenever you make changes to the configuration.

The program features tweaks only, and does not ship with options to handle Services, Tasks, or block Microsoft servers using the host file.

Windows Privacy Dashboard

Homepage: https://getwpd.com/

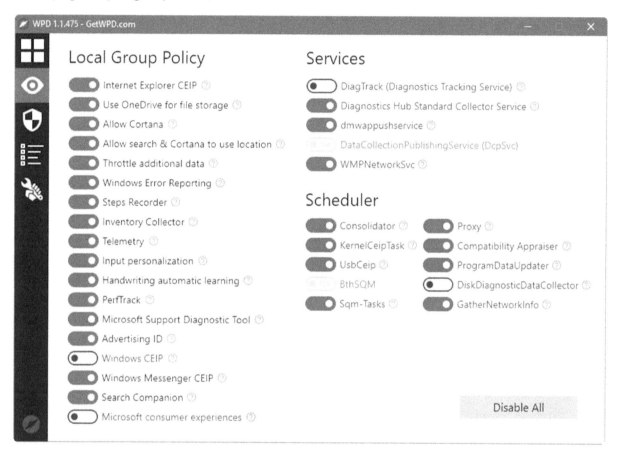

Windows Privacy Dashboard is another portable program for Windows 10 that provides you with options to manage privacy related preferences on Windows 10 machines.

The application displays the four groups privacy, firewall, apps and tweaker on start. Privacy is the main entry point when it comes to managing privacy using the program. It is divided into local group policy, services and scheduler options.

While most options are clear – Allow Cortana enables or disables the digital assistant for instance – some are not. That's where the question mark icon is put to use. Simply click on the question mark icon to display a detailed description of the selected entry.

Tweaker lists additional privacy related options, mostly what apps and may not interact with or use on the device.

Apps list all system apps that are distributed with Windows 10, and options to remove any of those from the Windows 10 machine.

Firewall finally provides you with options to block Telemetry, third-party apps and Windows Update connections.

RESOURCES

Windows Experience Blog

Our continuing commitment to your privacy with Windows 10: https://blogs.windows.com/windowsexperience/2017/01/10/continuing-commitment-privacy-windows-10/

Privacy and Windows 10 by Terry Myerson, Executive Vice President, Windows and Devices Group: https://blogs.windows.com/windowsexperience/2015/09/28/privacy-and-windows-10/

Privacy enhancements coming to the Windows 10 Fall Creators Update: https://blogs.windows.com/windowsexperience/2017/09/13/privacy-enhancements-coming-to-the-windows-10-fall-creators-update

Windows 10 privacy journey continues: more transparency and controls for you: https://blogs.windows.com/windowsexperience/2017/04/05/windows-10-privacy-journey-continues-more-transparency-and-controls-for-you/

Your feedback is helping shape Windows privacy: https://blogs.windows.com/windowsexperience/2017/08/07/feedback-helping-shape-windows-privacy/

General Pages of Interest

Microsoft Account Password Reset: https://account.live.com/password/reset

Microsoft Ads Opt-out: http://choice.microsoft.com/en-US/opt-out

Microsoft Privacy Statement: https://privacy.microsoft.com/en-us/privacystatement

Microsoft Services Agreement: https://www.microsoft.com/en/servicesagreement/

Microsoft Your Privacy: https://account.microsoft.com/privacy

Policy CSP: https://docs.microsoft.com/en-us/windows/client-management/mdm/policy-configuration-service-provider

Privacy at Microsoft: https://privacy.microsoft.com/en-US/

Microsoft Office

Manage privacy settings in Telemetry Dashboard (Office 2013): https://technet.microsoft.com/en-us/library/jj591589.aspx?f=255&MSPPError=-2147217396

Office 2013 Administrative Template Files and Office Customization Tool: https://www.microsoft.com/en-us/download/details.aspx?id=35554

Office 2016 Administrative Template Files and Office Customization Tool: https://www.microsoft.com/en-us/download/details.aspx?id=49030

Overview of Office Telemetry (Office 2013, Office 365 ProPlus): https://technet.microsoft.com/en-us/library/jj863580.aspx?f=255&MSPPError=-2147217396

Telemetry and Privacy

Configure Windows telemetry in your organization: https://docs.microsoft.com/en-us/windows/configuration/configure-windows-telemetry-in-your-organization

Deploy Windows Malicious Software Removal Tool in an enterprise environment: https://support.microsoft.com/en-us/help/891716/deploy-windows-malicious-software-removal-tool-in-an-enterprise-environment

Diagnostics, feedback and privacy in Windows 10: https://privacy.microsoft.com/en-us/windows-10-feedback-diagnostics-and-privacy

How to disable telemetry for Service Management Automation, Service Provider Foundation, and Service Manager Self-Serve Portal: https://support.microsoft.com/en-us/help/3096505/how-to-disable-telemetry-for-service-management-automation,-service-provider-foundation,-and-service-manager-self-serve-portal

Manage connections from Windows operating system components to Microsoft services: https://docs.microsoft.com/en-us/windows/configuration/manage-connections-from-windows-operating-system-components-to-microsoft-services

Manage Privacy: Windows Error Reporting and Resulting Internet Communication: https://technet.microsoft.com/en-us/library/jj618323(v=ws.11).aspx

Microsoft Trust Center – Windows telemetry privacy: https://www.microsoft.com/en-us/trustcenter/privacy/windows-telemetry-privacy-and-trust.aspx

Windows Error Reporting Settings: https://msdn.microsoft.com/en-us/library/windows/desktop/bb513638%28v=vs.85%29.aspx?f=255&MSPPError=-2147217396

Third-party Resources

Ask Woody: https://www.askwoody.com/

Born's Tech and Windows World: http://borncity.com/win/

Comparison of Windows 10 Privacy tools: https://www.ghacks.net/2015/08/14/comparison-of-windows-10-privacy-tools/

Ghacks Technology News: https://www.ghacks.net/

With Windows 10, Microsoft Blatantly Disregards User Choice and Privacy: A Deep Dive: https://www.eff.org/deeplinks/2016/08/windows-10-microsoft-blatantly-disregards-user-choice-and-privacy-deep-dive

Privacy Settings and Features

Connecting to open Wi-Fi hotspots in Windows 10: https://privacy.microsoft.com/en-us/windows-10-open-wi-fi-hotspots

General privacy settings in Windows 10: https://privacy.microsoft.com/en-us/general-privacy-settings-in-windows-10

Microsoft Edge, browsing data, and privacy: https://privacy.microsoft.com/en-US/windows-10-microsoft-edge-and-privacy

Opt out of location services: https://support.microsoft.com/en-us/help/20039/opt-out-of-location-services

Speech, inking, typing, and privacy https://privacy.microsoft.com/en-us/windows-10-speech-inking-typing-and-privacy-faq

Windows 10 Camera, Microphone and Privacy: https://privacy.microsoft.com/en-US/windows-10-camera-and-privacy

Windows 10 Location Service and privacy: https://privacy.microsoft.com/en-us/windows-10-location-and-privacy

Windows 10 privacy settings that apps use: https://privacy.microsoft.com/en-us/windows-10-privacy-settings-that-apps-use

Windows 10 Update Delivery Optimization: https://privacy.microsoft.com/en-US/windows-10-windows-update-delivery-optimization

Whitepapers and Docs

Available policies for Microsoft Edge: https://docs.microsoft.com/en-us/microsoft-edge/deploy/available-policies

Group Policies that apply only to Windows 10 Enterprise and Windows 10 Education: https://docs.microsoft.com/en-us/windows/client-management/group-policies-for-enterprise-and-education-editions

The Bones of the System: A Case Study of Logging and Telemetry at Microsoft: https://www.microsoft.com/en-us/research/wp-content/uploads/2016/02/ICSE-logging-submisson.pdf

Windows Server 2016 and System Center 2016 Telemetry: https://aka.ms/winservtelemetry

Windows 10, version 1703 basic level Windows diagnostic events and fields: https://docs.microsoft.com/en-us/windows/configuration/basic-level-windows-diagnostic-events-and-fields

Windows 10, version 1703 Diagnostic Data: https://docs.microsoft.com/en-us/windows/configuration/windows-diagnostic-data

INDEX

www.ingramcontent.com/pod-product-compliance
Lightning Source LLC
Chambersburg PA
CBHW080550060326
40689CB00021B/4803